Constructive education
for special groups:
handicapped and deviant children

*This is the third in the 'Constructive Education'
trilogy, the others being 'Constructive Education
for Children' and 'Constructive Education for
Adolescents'*

Constructive education for special groups: handicapped and deviant children

By W. D. Wall, B.A., Ph.D., F.B.Ps.S.

*Emeritus Professor of
Educational Psychology
in the University of London*

Harrap, London
unesco

First published in Great Britain 1979
by George G. Harrap & Co. Ltd
182–184 High Holborn, London WC1V 7AX
and the United Nations Educational,
Scientific and Cultural Organization,
7 Place de Fontenoy, 75700 Paris

© Unesco 1979

ISBN 0 245 53352 4

Phototypeset in V.I.P. Times by
Western Printing Services Ltd., Bristol
Printed in Great Britain by Biddles Ltd., Guildford

Preface

With the present level of development of the more industrialized countries it would seem that the resources are available to render daily life more independent for a larger number of the physically and mentally handicapped. Large-scale studies of the occurrence of handicap are still very few in number, and comprehensive national policies are often far from being laid down. After all, why should the handicapped not be expected to live stable and productive lives, lives that to a greater extent offer them the ability to survive on their own and to escape the fate of being 'institutionalized'?

This, the third volume of *Constructive education* . . . , completes Professor Wall's task of re-examining education with the pressing contemporary and future priorities in mind, in this particular case from the aspect of the handicapped and deviant child—'the casualties of our system'. The book puts forward many theses towards improving practice when dealing with this group of children, such as: (a) even though children may be grouped according to their handicap, all cases should be regarded as unique; (b) there is no sharp line marking the frontiers of handicap; (c) the importance of the family—and particularly the mother—in promoting the normal development of an otherwise handicapped child is often overlooked; (d) physical and mental handicap render the child so vulnerable to psychological handicap that deficit leads to deprivation; (e) placing physically and mentally handicapped children in ordinary schools should become more and more a widespread and socially acceptable solution.

The author reviews the prevalence of physical and mental handicap using a small number of recent surveys before defining the main groups of handicap and discussing the possibilities of ameliorating the child's way of life through education. He then goes on to examine the critical psychological influences on the child. A statement of the ways in which education and society may bring about tangible improvements in the identification and rehabilitation of children in this group leads on to an overview of the situation and a number of conclusions.

The Secretariat of the International Bureau of Education expresses once again its recognition of the author's unique knowledge. This work, although not necessarily expressing the views of Unesco, has examined the situation of handicapped, deprived and deviant children profoundly and with great compassion. It is to be hoped that Professor Wall's suggestions—the fruit of long experience—will make a lasting contribution to practice in dealing with the handicapped so that as many as possible can benefit from the joy of living.

Contents

Prefatory note

This last of the three volumes of *Constructive education* is a short survey of what we know about children who are, for a very great variety of reasons, thought to be sufficiently exceptional to warrant special educational consideration. However, the moment that we say this, its paradoxical incompleteness as a statement becomes apparent. There is no clear-cut line between the children and adolescents described and discussed in this book and those who form the population of our ordinary schools. All children are, in one way or another, exceptional, and all education, whether at home or in school, is or should be in some way special for each one. Our over-all concern is that of arranging, modifying and strengthening the educative environments in which the young grow up so that the experiences which they encounter at once satisfy their most profound needs and at the same time shape their learning in ways which fit them for the uncertain and changing future.

But the existence of a handicap, whether physical or social or both, sharply illuminates that process of interaction between a growing human being and the series of environments in which learning takes place. Because of this, it obliges us to look well beyond the formal processes of the school and very closely indeed at the key role of those—usually parents and other members of the family—who preside over the most intimate and emotional aspects of growth and whose influence on learning and the power to learn outweighs all others. And we see that the secrets of mental health, whether we think of this positively and generally or in the more restricted way that the term is often used, are to be sought in the complex tissue of human relations which are the vectors, as it were, along which growing children not only learn to construct their intelligence and their picture of the world, but to develop the styles and attitudes with which they will confront what life has to bring. Where, by disability of some kind, the child's own capacity to learn in constructive ways is prejudiced, we see very clearly indeed how important is the content and educative quality of the human environment in which he lives.

   It is only recently that we have come to accept in practice that children with physical or environmental handicaps are not a group apart, qualitatively different from the normal and mainly a subject for medical attention or social care. In many countries, and for some groups of the very severely handicapped in all countries, this lesson has still not been learned. Handicapped and even maladjusted children continue to be shut away and their lower than normal or different levels of functioning are accepted as inevitable and irremediable; they belong to a defined category. In many parts of the developing world, only the very severely handicapped are recognized by any form of special care or education and by far the majority of children with some impediment to their growth are to be found struggling along in ordinary schools—if indeed such schools exist. Pragmatically this may be the only possibility and, certainly historically, it was a stage in most of the countries of the Western world.

   However, as our knowledge of normal human development and of the interaction between biological and psychological growth has increased, we have become more aware of the impact of different kinds of handicap on the ways in which personality and cognition are shaped. This is leading us to a considerable shift of emphasis not only in the education of the handicapped themselves but, in fact, of the unhandicapped as well. We see that, though there are of course some whose defects or disabilities are of such a kind or degree of severity that for all practical purposes they are truly set apart, most children differ in degree rather than in kind from each other; and even of these differences, most can be traced to the result of normal processes of learning made different in their effects by a different physical or genetic apparatus, or by early environments themselves markedly different or not adequate to meet rather special circumstances.

   This notion provides the thesis not merely of this volume. What we have here is a continuation, extension and illustration of the ideas underlying the two previous volumes. Nor is the notion novel or as simple as it may seem; but it can be simply stated. In guiding human growth (and that is one of the main meanings of education) there are broad choices. We can educate—perhaps train would be a better word—for adjustment, making the best of what exists, and this will tend to be done in more or less authoritarian ways providing considerable security for learner and teacher. Or we can educate for adjustability, for flexibility. This is likely to be more difficult and will certainly involve, for the individual and for his or her educators, a higher level of anxiety since it does not give the security of learned solutions: it is intended to enable the individual to confront problems, perceive their novelty and devise personal solutions. Both styles have a further dimension, that of developing the individual's ability to learn (within the broad intentions of each) so far as is possible and, in either, this aspect of the task may be done more or less well. Both accept that the roots of many differences between people are probably genetic: the first, however, tends to take a rather more determinist view than the second, which points to the great malleability of human beings and seeks to find ways of maintaining and enhancing flexibility through lifelong processes of increasingly autonomous learning.

The more authoritarian and conservative style easily lends itself to the acceptance of a separate education for specified groups held to be different—for the handicapped, for children of different social classes or of different ethnic groups. The more open style, though possibly overly optimistic in much the same way as the nineteenth century, *l'éducation peut tout*, stresses the integration of all groups on the assumption that, where differences are inferiorities, they are remediable and that all human beings are capable of a higher development than, in general, we see.

It is the second general view then that leads in this book to the continual stress upon normality as an aim—not the normality of uniformity, but that which falls within the wide range of acceptable individual differences—and upon the maintenance of handicapped children so far as is possible within the general run of the social and educational life of their unhandicapped fellows. Two consequences are then sought. The first is that even the quite severely handicapped will not become cut off from the general life of the community but share equally in it, profiting from a general tolerance of difference. The second is that any efforts made to individualize education so that some at least of the worst deprivations of handicap may be compensated for, if not remedied, will have a backwash effect upon the environments provided at school and at home for the so-called normal.

One of the strange facts stumbled upon while writing this book is that apparently there have been very few attempts indeed over the past decade, at an official, governmental level, to look comprehensively at the whole area of handicap in all its educational and other implications. There have been the two reports by Unesco covering the state of play, as it were, in a number of countries (see Chapter II, note 72); there is the volume edited by the National Children's Bureau in the United Kingdom and cited in Chapter III, p. 65. But so far as I have been able to trace, the only official national effort to look again at handicap and to review the field at the level of public policy is that of the Warnock Committee in the United Kingdom.* When we think of the immense public interest which has been displayed in many countries of the world in the reform of formal education, in the curriculum, in what is called lifelong education, in higher education and almost every other aspect of the public systems we set up for the young, this is very surprising. There has been no lack of research concerned with particular handicapped groups—the field is very rich; but few efforts have been made at the kind of synthesis necessary to verify whether our policies are apt or should be improved. This is disquieting since it suggests that the handicapped are still excluded from the general educational considerations of administrators and politicians, who think of these groups of children, adolescents and adults as inhabitants of some secret garden or ghetto to which only 'specialists' have the key.

To some readers, it may seem surprising that the question of the training of teachers for work with the handicapped or deviant clubs has not been, except incidentally, dealt with in this volume. The reason for this is that, in the

* See appendix, p.137

writer's view, this training is logically, and should be practically, a part of general teacher training. Similarly, the training of the psychologist and the organization of psychological services for the handicapped should not be separated from other aspects of the work. The reader will therefore find in chapters 7 and 8 of *Constructive education for adolescents* a full treatment of these matters.

May I end by thanking the many colleagues who read parts of this book in its various stages, my own students, themselves experienced teachers of the handicapped, and those parents and handicapped children who over the years have taught me some of the human dimensions of the problems dealt with here. To them, to Mrs Anne Honeyman and Mrs Jean Day who lightened the burdens of writing, my warmest thanks are due.

W.D.W.
Burnham, Bucks.
April 1978

Chapter one

The prevalence and educational consequence of physical disability

In Europe and North America, since the turn of the century, there has been a considerable increase in our knowledge of and provision for various handicapping conditions affecting children. Our understanding of how disabling conditions may come about through a great variety of antenatal and perinatal conditions—the effects of drugs, of diet, of physiological conditions in the mother, and in the mechanics of childbirth itself—has led to measures to prevent the occurrence of many conditions, or at least to minimize their incidence and consequences. Improved nutrition, improved environmental sanitation and a general rise in standards of living, including a more widespread knowledge of the health and nutritional needs of children and mothers, has brought about a more generally healthy community, decreased the infant mortality rate and greatly diminished the post-natal causes of handicapping physical conditions.

But something else has happened too. The generally improved services for expectant and young mothers, the elimination of some of the causes of death and disablement in infancy, has led to a higher survival rate among children with both severe and marginal handicaps, notably those with damage to the central nervous system, and to a more prolonged life in other groups who tended to die in the first two decades of life—for example, so-called 'mongol' children (Down's syndrome) many of whom now survive well into the third decade. Another example is that of children born with spina bifida, about half of whom survive to enjoy adult lives of almost normal length.

We have understood and, to a large extent, controlled some of the commoner causes of handicap—for example cerebral palsy (maternal rubella, rhesus incompatibility) or blindness due to retrolental fibroplasia (caused by excessive administration of oxygen at birth). But advances in pharmacology have been accompanied by accidents—for example, the side effects of streptomycin in the treatment of measles or of thalidomide taken by pregnant mothers—which have given rise to new disabilities or deformities. Of some disabilities we are only recently becoming aware—in differentiating, for example, some kinds of afferent or efferent communication difficulties from broad miscellaneous categories like 'mental defect'. Others, like some disturbances of the enzyme or hormonal systems, which were either not detected in the past or thought to be incurable, have now become amenable to treatment and, if detected early enough, have little or no bearing upon the subsequent course of general development.

Perhaps the most important change is not concerned with primary prevention or physical treatment. It is the beginning of a subtle change in our thinking about how to minimize the effects of disability. The early history of provision for handicapped children, and too much of what takes place even now, is predicated upon at least a tacit assumption that the child with a defect in his physical or sensory apparatus, or who appears to develop intellectually much more slowly than his peers, is in some way clearly different from 'normal' children, almost as if he came from a different species. This carries over into another assumption: that somehow there is a direct, necessary and one-to-one causal relationship between, say, the fact that a child cannot see and his general ability to learn, his personality and his character, and that his emotional and educational needs are different *in kind* from those of his sighted fellows. Many handicapped children, when they are seen in school, certainly seem to be different, and a high proportion are backward and dull. This is still too often accepted as an inevitable part of the disability itself and many special schools and institutions tend to act in consequence. For example, they stress an education with manual (and often out-of-date) vocations in view, emphasizing training rather than broad cultural and cognitive development in their curricula for all handicapped children in their charge. A high proportion of children, often with complex handicaps but sometimes with only one major but not clearly understood difficulty, have also been regarded as totally ineducable and consigned to institutions where little in the way of education, training or sometimes even of occupation is available.

It is, of course, true that a very small proportion of children indeed is so severely damaged at birth that the most devoted and enlightened care and attention will do little more than arouse a few small flickers of intelligence. There are others—for example, children who are born blind and deaf—whose handicaps seem, and are, exceedingly difficult to overcome even to a mild degree and then only by a huge effort of patience, insight and knowledge in those around them. The handicaps of others very severely modify, under any circumstances we can imagine, the kinds of expectations that can be set for their development as children and their hopes of an approximately normal adult life.

But it must again be emphasized that these cases are proportionately few, even in comparison with the numbers of children who have some sort of handicap of a less manifestly serious kind. For most of those labelled as 'handicapped', the impairment or disability does not directly affect the central nervous system in a massive way; most defects are peripheral, impinging upon sight or hearing, or locomotion, or affect general physical robustness. Such impairments may certainly interfere with learning and the growth of intelligence, but this is largely because they make many kinds of interaction with the human and material environment more difficult and may make some of the usual forms of essential interaction practically impossible. The corollary to this is not that such children are doomed to a deprived existence, but that an insightful series of modifications of the environment itself should be made to meet fundamental growth needs in a different way. Of course, it may not be possible to devise fully adequate substitute situations, but a careful programme beginning as soon after birth as possible and continuing throughout the main developmental period can at least greatly diminish, if not entirely compensate for, the impediments to learning imposed by the handicap. The picture of physical defect or disability automatically implying intellectual, social, educational and emotional handicap, through an accumulating deviation from the normal paths of development, is one that begins to change radically once we plan help—to parent and child—on the assumption that the needs of a handicapped baby, infant, school child or adolescent are intrinsically no different, just because he is handicapped, from those of anyone else.

An acceptance, in actual practice and in detail, that the real threat to development comes not generally from the physical defect itself, but from the way in which it interferes with learning and deprives a child of vital experiences which ordinary children get as a matter of course, has another implication. It should lead those around him to drop the spurious causal mystique of diagnostic labels and the often blindly consequential treatment which follows. Instead of categorizing such children and treating them as if they were of another species, the emphasis should be upon normality and an imaginative attempt at ensuring the best possible development by a deliberate manipulation of the environment in which they grow.

THREE STUDIES OF THE PREVALENCE AND EFFECTS OF HANDICAP

Although we have suggested that the attitude outlined above is beginning to penetrate into practice, particularly in connection with, for example, the deaf, it is far from universally accepted and applied. And this for a variety of reasons.

At least one of these is that the picture we have of the prevalence and of the impact of handicap is confused and incomplete. There are, for example, great differences from country to country in the criteria used for defining handicap, in the descriptive and diagnostic labels used, and in the availability and quality of services. Even within one country, the assignment of children to particular groups according to the kinds of difficulty or defect from which they suffer, varies more or less arbitrarily according to the views of those making the classification and according to the purpose for which the classification is made.

This makes attempts at comparable assessments of prevalence in different countries and different parts of the world hazardous. There are also real differences between countries in the prevalence of handicaps related to great differences in the provision of health, educational and social services. Different levels of nutrition, of antenatal and perinatal care, and differing styles of child rearing all have an effect to increase or decrease the hazards of gestation, birth, infant mortality and vulnerability, and consequently on the numbers and kinds of damage or disability which occur. The attitudes of families and communities, and particularly their kinds and levels of tolerance of deviation from what is held to be normal for their society, all play their part. Thus we find real and substantial difference between say northern and southern Europe, between North and South America and between the developed and the developing world.

What we can do, however, is to examine the magnitude of the problem and its bearing upon individual children in some countries whose primary preventive services are comparatively highly developed and which also have social and educational services designed to provide for the handicapped. Even in such countries, however, there have been few fully adequate and comprehensive epidemiological studies; nor are they based upon very clearly defined criteria of the kind implied above. They provide a sobering snapshot of a state of affairs which is far from ideal. They reveal that not only do we not apply the educational lessons which we are beginning to learn, but that, even where the provision made is apparently rich and varied, very many children are not catered for in any suitable way.[1] We may illustrate this from recent research conducted by Rutter, Tizard and Whitmore in the United Kingdom.[2] It concerns all the children aged between 9 and 12 in the Isle of Wight, an area representative of England generally, which is a country with a long history of special education and with junior schools as flexible and child-centred as any to be found in Europe. One may therefore reasonably say that it represents at least a fairly average picture, although in decaying inner-city areas in England the situation is probably very much worse, as it would almost certainly be in the less-developed countries.[3]

These workers found one child in six (16 per cent)[4] to have a chronic handicap of moderate or severe intensity. The proportions of the intellectually retarded (2·6 per cent) could be considered as quite usual, but the authors add that one-third of these had a neurological disorder. Adopting a very severe criterion for reading backwardness they found that 7·9 per cent of all pupils were twenty-eight months or more behind what would be expected of their chronological age; 3·7 per cent were similarly retarded compared with their general ability. Eight per cent of those with reading difficulties and 24 per cent of the intellectually retarded had *marked* emotional and behavioural disorders. Of all pupils, 5·4 per cent[5] were held to have clinically significant psychiatric conditions; 5·5 per cent of children had chronic physical handicaps of which asthma was the most common (2·3 per cent) and these children tended to be more emotionally disturbed than others. A quarter of the handicapped children had more than one handicap, and 1 per cent of all children had three or more handicaps (5·2 per cent of handicapped).

A proportion of one child in six apparently requiring some form of special attention presents an enormous problem—approximately half-a-million such children in English schools, or something like an average of six in every ordinary class, if no provision were made elsewhere. It must also be remembered that the criteria used were primarily medical, though not exclusively. They certainly excluded many minor social and personal handicaps—mild dullness, social need and deprivation, visual-motor disorders, developmental lags—which constitute in many individuals severe impediments to learning. Therefore, it is perhaps surprising, and certainly disturbing, to find that, for example, of the total of 10 per cent who were discovered to be intellectually handicapped or severely backward in reading, only one-third were receiving any form of special help, half of them in special schools and half in special classes in ordinary schools. 'Most of the children with reading difficulties received no kind of special help in reading'.[6] Of those children with alleged psychiatric conditions (5·4 per cent) only one in five was receiving treatment, and in nine cases out of ten the difficulties had not been expertly diagnosed in spite of a well-established medical service. Of the clearly physically handicapped, one in three were not being satisfactorily helped with their educational and emotional problems.

THE EDUCATIONAL CONSEQUENCES—A FRENCH SURVEY

A complementary picture of the actuality of physical handicap comes from France.[7] It consists of a survey carried out in 1966 and 1967 of all physically handicapped and chronically sick children (excluding the intellectually retarded and seriously defective) known to clinics, hospitals and voluntary organizations in the area of Nancy–Metz. Four years later, in 1970–71, the same team conducted a follow-up study of some 650 of the children, of whom some 520 were still at school. It is again a primarily medical-paediatric study with disadvantages similar to those of the Isle of Wight survey.

In the *département* of Meurthe et Moselle, which is the background to the study, the workers estimate that handicapped children and young people under 20 amount to 2·65 per cent[8] of the age group, of whom a little more than 1 per cent are intellectually retarded, 0·2 per cent have sensory handicaps, 0·5 per cent are physically handicapped or delicate, and 0·7 per cent are psychiatrically disturbed; 58·6 per cent of all handicapped children have at least one other handicap. More than a quarter of the physically handicapped are impaired in their motor development; the rest consist of categories like asthma, diabetes, heart anomalies, epilepsy etc. However, in the initial survey three-quarters of the children actually selected for study were motor handicapped, and it was only these who were followed up in 1970–71.

At the time of the initial survey, over 90 per cent of the children were in school—67 per cent attending daily, 11 per cent being day boarders, 8 per cent in boarding schools for ordinary children, 9 per cent in special boarding schools. Of the 9 per cent not in school at all, a small number were being educated by correspondence. The most striking (if not unexpected) finding is the degree of educational retardation among the generality of the handicapped studied. Only 42 per cent were in grades for their age, 28 per cent were one year and 30 per cent two or more years behind.[9] The proportions of relative failure and backwardness vary with the categories of handicap; for example, of poliomyelitic children, 27 per cent were one year behind and 21 per cent two or more; of orthopaedic cases, 22 per cent one year and 30 per cent more than three years behind the normal; of the cerebrally palsied, 80 per cent were retarded educationally and only 20 per cent progressing normally. Sixty-two per cent of the total motor-impaired group had an intelligence quotient of 80 or better (more than a third had an I.Q. of 100-plus) but only 34 per cent finished a complete primary schooling without being at least a year behind. Only the asthmatics showed an educational achievement which could be regarded as satisfactory—78 per cent of them being in the correct year for their age or not more than a year behind, a figure slightly better than that for the general run of unhandicapped children—and this in spite of multiple and prolonged absences from school. In all groups of handicapped, fewer children proceeded to selective forms of secondary education than was usual for the population as a whole.

Various comparisons were made between the educational status of handicapped children and that of their non-handicapped siblings. In general, the group of normal brothers and sisters presented the same picture as any children, i.e. it seemed to be the handicap rather than the socio-economic situation of the family which was concerned in the relative failure of the handicapped group. As the authors of the various papers note, this is the reverse of what should be. The object of medical science, they assert, is to cure or compensate for a physical anomaly or deficit; the object of education is to prevent so far as possible the deficit from becoming a handicap—socially, economically and personally. In fact, to compensate for a physical disability, a child or young person should be helped to be more successful in education than his peers. These children were markedly less so.

The nature of the problem facing schools and families with physically handicapped children is vividly depicted by a few other figures from this survey: about 2 per cent of the motor handicapped had so slight an impediment that only general medical supervision was held to be necessary; 75 per cent could, without major difficulties and with suitable prostheses, follow an ordinary school day; a further 5 per cent were capable of attending an ordinary school but only if special adaptations were made; 7–11 per cent were either at home or in a specialized centre. Seventy-six per cent of the children had been hospitalized at least once, and more than half of them a number of times; only 51 per cent had been able on coming out of hospital to stay in a re-education centre for convalescence and remedial education in order to catch up what they had lost. Thus, although this handicapped group is disadvantaged in many ways and presents considerable management problems for families and to some extent for the schools, there seems to be little inherent reason why normal educational progress should not have been made, except that insufficient attention had been devoted to alleviating the *additional* hindrances imposed on the child's learning by absence, fatigue, diminished mobility, and so on.

Manciaux and his colleagues at Nancy suggest that some of the reasons for the general educational retardation of handicapped children may lie in the home, not so much because the families are themselves abnormal as because they are insufficiently aware of a handicapped child's special needs. In general, 69 per cent or more of parents were regarded as 'normal' in their handling so far as care and affection went. In 24 per cent of families, while the emotional climate was good, a lack of realism led the parents not to understand the child's needs. Only 7 per cent of families were regarded as having a bad effect. A frequent observation, however, was that families tended to over-protect their handicapped children, to be ready to condone school absences and to fail sufficiently to stress the importance of catching up lost time. Moreover, it was found that the educational difficulties generally are the more marked the earlier the onset of the handicap, since it interferes with normal emotional and intellectual exchanges, inhibits locomotion and so on. In over 50 per cent of the cases, onset was at birth or in the first year, with a further 14 per cent between the first and fifth year. Only 5 per cent of the children became handicapped after the age of 11. Significantly, the writers note that medical staff are insufficiently acquainted with the problems of education and upbringing, and are unable to give the kind of advice and support families and schools need. It is also clear that, for a variety of reasons, the schools do not, or cannot, undertake sufficient remedial and supportive work to enable most handicapped children to keep pace with their fellows. Similarly, handicapped children are frequently obliged to travel longish distances to school without help; only rarely does account seem to be taken at home and in school of their greater susceptibility to fatigue, of the psychological effects imposed on some by their inability to take part in physical education and games of various kinds—indeed of the many apparently minor ways in which a handicap, not serious in itself, may operate to deprive or single out a child.

THE FOLLOW-UP: THE EFFECTS OF SPECIAL SCHOOLING

Undertaken in the school year 1970–71, the follow-up concerned 650 motor-handicapped children who had been surveyed in 1966–67, of whom 520 were still in schools of one kind or another. Among them 45 per cent were poliomyelitic; 32 per cent were orthopaedically handicapped; and 23 per cent cerebrally palsied. Two-thirds of the group were either fully independent or very nearly so, 25 per cent were sufficiently mobile to climb stairs, and 8 per cent were dependent for mobility to various degrees on others (most of them cerebral palsied children). According to a complete evaluation of their condition (including the use of upper limbs, and associated handicaps) 81 per cent were considered medically to be capable of a normal home and school life, 6 per cent were capable of adjustment with an adaptation of the ordinary environment, 10 per cent needed a special environment (most of them cerebral palsied). Only 1 per cent were judged ineducable, and fully dependent.

In 1966–67, 88 per cent of these motor-handicapped children had been attending ordinary schools; by 1970 the proportion had fallen to 70 per cent. Of the children in specialized provision in 1966–67 (12 per cent), six out of every ten had been in special classes attached to ordinary schools, whereas by

1970, seven out of every ten were in separate special schools or in institutions. During the interval of four years the number of specialized institutions in France had more than doubled, as had the total number of children in them. It was also found that the number of handicapped in classes normal for their age had fallen from 44 per cent in 1966 to 30 per cent in 1970, with a considerable increase (from 23 per cent in 1966 to 36 per cent in 1970) in those who were two or more years retarded. Again, over the period of four years, although 44 per cent of the handicapped had got no worse educationally, 43 per cent had deteriorated by at least one year and one-third by two or more years. Only 13 per cent actually 'improved' but this improvement was largely apparent only because they had entered transitional classes or left for another kind of school.

This French experience demonstrates what has been found elsewhere—that an expansion of specialized *separate* provision for handicap tends to draw into itself children who might be as well or better off in ordinary schools, or in special classes attached to primary or secondary schools. Furthermore, it seems that, if the handicapped are not to add an accumulating educational retardation to their physical disadvantages, they need discriminating, but discrete, special help and guidance at critical points in their development: in very early childhood, in the pre-school years, and subsequently towards the end of the primary school and first years of the secondary school. Merely syphoning them off into special schools does not, in itself, ensure better progress—in fact it may do the reverse. The evidence also seems to suggest that, in the families themselves, among the various medical and social professionals, and among educationists, prejudiced attitudes, stereotypes and sheer ignorance of what it is possible for a handicapped individual to achieve are at work to prevent the fullest realization of human potential—indeed, that there are pressures towards over-protection and under-achievement which have to be understood and actively combated.

EDUCATION IN ORDINARY SCHOOLS

A study by Anderson,[10] this time of the adaptation and progress of ninety-nine handicapped children being educated in ordinary infant (5–7 years) and junior (7–11+ years) schools in southern England, adds a further gloss. The children selected were fairly typical of those normally placed in special schools or classes for physically handicapped. Hence, those children with only slight handicaps were excluded from the research sample, as were physically handicapped, intellectually retarded children. The junior school pupils studied (seventy-four children) were classified in three groups: the *mildly handicapped* (17·5 per cent) who had no major physical/motor problem and not more than four minor physical problems and, on the behavioural/communication side, not more than four difficulties; the *moderately handicapped* (60·8 per cent) who had one, and not more than three, major physical/motor problems and not more than six major problems altogether; and the *severely handicapped* (21·6 per cent) who had more than three major physical/motor problems or more than six major problems overall. The biggest symptomatic groups were the cerebrally palsied (21·6 per cent), spina bifida (16·2 per cent), congenital abnormalities (24·3 per cent), and a miscellaneous category (27 per cent). The infant group (twenty-five children) had less variety in handicap, with the biggest category being spina bifida with hydrocephalus; all were rated moderately or severely handicapped. Placement in a special class, unit or school had been suggested for seventeen (68 per cent) of the twenty-five infant school pupils and for 60 per cent of the junior group, nearly 10 per cent of whom had been transferred from some kind of special to ordinary schooling.

Anderson found that the majority of parents favoured placement in ordinary schools, and often had had to fight hard to convince the authorities that this should be permitted. The children, although (proportionally to the severity of their handicap) less physically and socially independent than control groups of unhandicapped pupils in the same schools, were as independent as their handicaps allowed; ordinary school placement appeared to act as a stimulus to independence. Eighty per cent of the infants and 73 per cent of the juniors appeared to be making a good adjustment to their disabilities. As far as behaviour disorders were concerned, fewer of the handicapped (14 per cent) group had behaviour problems than of the controls (19 per cent) according to their teachers, and the highest rate of deviant behaviour (25 per cent) was in the neurologically abnormal group. The most significant item educationally is the short concentration span reported by the teachers in 88 per cent of the cerebrally palsied, 43 per cent of the other handicapped and 35 per cent of the controls. In general, too, 66·6 per cent of the physically handicapped without neurological damage were rated as 'well adjusted' to school as compared to 72 per cent of controls.

In terms of I.Q., the physically handicapped without neurological abnormality were similar to their normal controls, but the neurologically abnormal had (non-verbal) scores clustering between I.Q. 70 and 90. In arithmetic and in reading, this neurologically abnormal group was markedly below average and not solely for reasons of lower ability. The other physically handicapped did not differ greatly either in reading or in arithmetic from the controls, although there were a few more *markedly* low attainers among them.

Anderson concludes that most children, even those with very marked physical handicaps, are, with some extra help, well able to cope with and benefit from the curriculum of an ordinary school, provided there is no neurological abnormality. However, for the neurologically abnormal, extra help seems critical if their development and education are not to suffer. In fact the crucial problem is not physical handicap as such but the existence of learning disorder.

CONCLUSION

In complementary ways the three studies cited sharpen up the picture of handicap. Even in favourable circumstances, at least one child in six has a disability of some magnitude—and the figure would probably be higher if defects which seem medically slight but which constitute a grave handicap to learning are included. The French survey, and to some extent the work done in the Isle of Wight, underline two things: (a) all too many disabled children fall behind educationally even in ordinary schools, for lack of any special supportive arrangements to minimize the effects of their handicap; and (b) transferring them to special schools and institutions does not necessarily improve their chances. Indeed, the work of Anderson suggests the reverse—that quite severely physically handicapped children can thrive like other children in a good infant and primary school. Finally, there is the strong suggestion from the French survey that much of the developmental and educational retardation which marked their groups must be traced to the fact that few of the medical, social and educational staff in contact with the families had been able to give the understanding advice and help—not only of a medical or material kind, but psychological and educational as well—which is clearly needed.

NOTES

1. Commission on Emotional and Learning Disorders in Children. *One million children*: the CELDIC report. Toronto, published by Leonard Crainford for the Commission . . ., 1970. Commission sur l'étude des troubles de l'affectivité et de l'apprentissage chez l'enfant. *Un million d'enfants*: le rapport CELDIC. Toronto, publié par Leonard Crainford pour la Commission . . ., 1970.
2. Rutter, M.; Tizard, J.; Whitmore, K. *Education, health and behaviour*. London, Longman, 1970.
3. In view of the association of many forms of handicap, particularly the milder grades of intellectual retardation, with social conditions, some schools in poor areas will have a very much higher proportion than others. The epidemiological study made in the Isle of Wight was repeated in certain of its aspects in an Inner-London borough, itself reasonably typical of London as a whole. It was found that emotional disorder, conduct disorder and specific reading difficulty were all at least twice as common among the 10-year-old London children as among those from the Isle of Wight. The authors suggest that these higher rates of prevalence are due in part to: (a) high proportions of marital discord and disruption in the London families, many parents showing mental disorder and antisocial behaviour; (b) many more families in poor social circumstances; (c) the London schools are more often character-ized by high staff (and pupil) turnover. (Rutter, M., et al. Attainment and adjustment in two geographical areas. I: The prevalence of psychiatric disorder. *Br. j. psychiatr.* (Ashford, Kent), vol. 126, 1975, p. 493–509; Rutter, M. et al. Geographical areas. II: The prevalence of specific reading retardation. *Br. j. psychiatr.* (Ashford, Kent), vol. 126, 1975, p. 510–19; Rutter, M, et al. Attainment and adjustment in two geographical areas. III: Some factors accounting for area differences. *Br. j. psychiatr.* (Ashford, Kent), vol. 126, 1975, p. 520–33.)
   Similarly, R. N. Jackson (Urban distribution of educable mental handicap. *J. ment. def. res.* (London, National Society for Mentally Handicapped Children), vol. 12, pt. 4, Dec. 1968) found that prevalence rates per 1,000 varied in the twenty-three Wards of the City of Edinburgh from 14·6 to 0·7. A Belgian study of records kept over a decade in the urban industrial region of La Louvière (Cordier, J. *Contribution à l'épidémiologie de la débilité mentale*. Bruxelles, Edns. de l'Institut de Sociologie, 1963) suggests that the profoundly and severely subnormal, most of whom had neurological damage, came from all social groups, but in the case of other subnormal children, particularly where one of the parents was subnormal, many came from socially and economically unfavourable backgrounds, as did the 5–9 per cent of pupils who did not pass the five primary grades by the time they had completed eight years of school attendance.
4. F. Brenner (*Das behinderte Kind in der Berliner und Wiener Sonderschule*. Berlin-Charlottenburg, Carl Marhold Verlagsbuchhandlung, 1967) states that the proportion

catered for in special schools and classes in Berlin and Vienna is about 7·5 per cent of the school population. Probably omitted from this are children whose main or only problem is a moderate or severe degree of educational subnormality.

Mainar, G. Gonzalvo (*Educación especial*. Madrid, Ediciones Movata, 1967) claims that a quarter of children of school age fall into this category. A report, quoted in the Council of Europe's *Newsletter*, no. 3, 1972, of the Conference of Ministers of Education, March 1972, gives the total proportion of handicapped children in the Federal Republic of Germany as 7·65 per cent. The largest categories mentioned are: serious learning difficulties, 4 per cent; maladjusted, 1 per cent; mentally handicapped, 0·6 per cent; blind, 0·01 per cent; deaf, 0·05 per cent; physically handicapped, 0·2 per cent; hard-of-hearing, 0·18 per cent; partially sighted, 0·1 per cent; speech defective, 0·4 per cent. The fifth five-year plan in France estimates that 12 per cent of the population aged 5–19 is in some way handicapped. The military medical examiners reject 8·5 per cent of those called to the colours. See Manciaux, M.; Rauber, C. Problèmes et solutions. *In*: Manciaux, M., ed. Scolarisation des enfants handicapés physiques et malades chroniques en milieu scolaire normal. *Sauvegarde de l'enfance* (Paris, Association française pour la sauvegarde de l'enfance et de l'adolescence), 22e année, no. 7, septembre 1967, p. 297–303.

5. A check carried out by the research team suggested that something like 20 per cent of cases may have been missed and the true figure should be 6·8 per cent.

6. Rutter, M.; Tizard, J.; Whitmore, K. op cit., (p. 51–3) note 2.

7. The inspiration and general direction came from Professor Michel Manciaux, professor of paediatrics at Nancy, but from the outset many of his colleagues in the university, the medical and social services and the education system were closely involved. The principal publications to date are: Manciaux, M., ed. op. cit., note 4; Manciaux, M.; About, P. J. Scolarisation des enfants handicapés physiques et malades chroniques en milieu scolaire normal. *Sauvegarde de l'enfance* (Paris, AFSEA), 23e année, no. 8, oct. 1968; and Manciaux, M. *Scolarité des jeunes handicapés* [Mimeo. Nancy, 1974?]. Further accounts are to be found in two doctoral theses (medicine) of the University of Nancy by A. M. Meyer (1967) and C. Gegout (1974).

8. These figures are somewhat lower than those of the Isle of Wight survey, probably because of differences in methods of case-finding and diagnosis, and real demographic differences. There are, too, well established differences between countries in incidence of defects and malformations at birth (ranging from over 2 per cent to less than 1 per cent), in the incidence of particular defects (for example, in Northern Ireland, central nervous system defect is three times as frequent as in Australia) and in survival rates. (See WHO table cited by Rumeau-Roquette, C.; Etienne, C. Epidémiologie des malformations congénitales. *In*: Mande, R.; Masse, N.; Manciaux, M. *Pédiatrie sociale*. Paris, Flammarion, 1972.) The survival rates are highest for deformations and defects of limbs and lowest for central nervous system damage. In all, something like 3–4 per cent of the National Child Development Study's 1958 cohort suffered from or developed serious defects; two-fifths of these die before age 7, leaving 2·6 per cent with defects of a serious or potentially serious nature detectable at this age. (See Davie, R.; Butler, N.; Goldstein, H. *From birth to seven*: second report of the National Child Development Study. London, Longman, 1972. Chapter XIII.)

9. Official figures cited by the authors suggest that, of pupils in general, 68 per cent are normal in grade for their age, 20 per cent one year behind, and 12 per cent 2+ years behind.

10. Anderson, Elizabeth Marion. *The disabled school child*. London, Methuen, 1973.

Chapter two

The principal groups of the mentally and physically handicapped

INTRODUCTION

We have so far spoken of the prevalence and some of the consequences of disability in fairly broad terms, much as though a defect or a handicap had similar effects whatever its kind, cause or severity. This is to some extent true as a generalization; but in practice defects or disabilities of different kinds propose different problems for the child himself and for those who deal with his care and education and, although consequences are always potentially serious, they do not, as has been emphasized, necessarily correspond in any direct way to the severity of the effects we see on the child's general development. It will therefore be of interest briefly to review the main broad categories of handicap. First we will look at that large group of children whose main presenting difficulty is a general slowness in learning—those who are intellectually and educationally subnormal (shown in Table 1, p. 23)—remembering always that marked slowness in learning and many of the numerically most frequent forms of subnormality may be secondary consequences of other handicapping conditions or associated with them, including conditions almost uniquely attributable to deficiencies in the child's early environment. We can then go on to consider disabilities affecting the special senses, general physical health and locomotion and those in which damage or anomaly in the cerebral cortex is the principal defect.

THE INTELLECTUALLY RETARDED AND DULL

PROFOUNDLY, SEVERELY AND MODERATELY INTELLECTUALLY RETARDED CHILDREN

The most obvious deviation, and one of those earliest provided for, is that of marked retardation in mental growth. It frequently complicates other handicaps and is complicated by them. The profoundly, severely and moderately retarded (the 'idiots' and 'imbeciles' as they used to be called), whose mental development is so slow that their progress is less than half that of the child of average ability, are nearly always detected soon after birth or at the latest in the pre-school period. In all, such children amount to about 3 per 1,000 of the population, of whom a large proportion are, in the true sense, 'defective'; that is, they are genuinely pathological cases of genetic,[1] perinatal,[2] or environmentally caused[3] defect. A few suffer from no demonstrable pathological disturbance and seem to be at the extreme of a normal distribution of ability. With the exception of conditions caused by defects of endocrine function (for example in the thyroid), or of metabolic function (for example phenylketonuria or galactosemia), at present little can be done medically or otherwise to raise their level of potential ability.[4] The problem is that of devising an upbringing and an education which will enable them to make the best use of their very limited capacity. A very small proportion, it is true, seem to be so feebly endowed, or so organically or emotionally disturbed, as to be incapable of forming even the most elementary type of habits, and at present all that can be done for them is to provide a humane care to prevent damage to themselves or to others. The majority, however, can be taught to feed and clothe themselves, to become to a moderate degree socialized, and even to undertake the simplest forms of industrial occupation. They will only rarely be self-supporting; most will not learn to read even the simplest words or to make the simplest calculations. Yet, there is evidence to show that many more of them are at least trainable[5] than are at present trained.

What is perhaps even more important is the growing realization that some children find themselves classified in this group even though they have potentialities such that they are educable to a fairly marked degree. Many children with cerebral lesions, with so severe a hearing impairment that, unhelped, they become effectively dumb, or who have grave difficulties in communication, still find themselves consigned to the 'ineducable' group. More and more, however, skilled differential diagnosis and developing methods of compensation for physical or sensory deficits by educational means are leading to the recuperation of such children—often with surprising results.

It is true that most of these children cannot be placed among their normal fellows, but it is regrettable that even now they are completely excluded from the education systems in many countries; and, as a consequence, cut off from anything but strictly medical and custodial care. They are frequently placed in hospitals for adults without the skilled staff to give the systematic training which could markedly improve their lives and could carry them beyond the merely vegetative existence into which, lacking stimulation, they only too readily sink. Others are in day-care centres set up mainly to provide some relief to the parents.[6]

CHILDREN WITH DOWN'S SYNDROME OR 'MONGOLS'

Before we leave this intellectually retarded group, a word should be said about a special sub-group which has assumed greater importance numerically of recent years. There is a considerable number of children who are born with chromosomal anomalies; very few indeed survive, with the exception of those called popularly from their general appearance 'mongols'. About 0·4–0·6 per cent of births are of this kind, mostly to mothers considerably older than average, and often at the end of a line of normal siblings.[7] Such children in the past died very early in life and rarely survived adolescence; now the chances of survival well into the second or third decade of life and longer are greatly improved. At present, of all 10-year-olds, a little over 1 per 1,000 is a mongol.

Usually they are at least moderately retarded intellectually, with I.Q.s only occasionally higher than 50; few are in the profoundly or severely retarded categories. They tend, in contrast to the retarded generally, to enjoy better health and to have fewer physical disabilities—for example epilepsy is uncommon. There is little evidence that as a group they differ in temperament from other intellectually retarded children, though because of their relatively slightly higher intelligence and social ability and because of their reasonably good health they present many fewer problems of management. Consequently, proportionally more of them live at home, with advantage, since the social development of retarded children at home tends to be superior to that of similar children in institutions.[8]

Like other retarded children, mongols have difficulty in learning to speak, may show relative unresponsiveness to the human voice[9] and need considerable careful stimulation to learn to communicate in this way.

'AUTISTIC' CHILDREN[10]

Another group, generally differentiated from the subnormal and which has aroused interest recently, is the so-called 'autistic'. A small number of children (1:2,500), in most cases for no apparently organic reason (though some have other handicaps), fail to learn to communicate or develop social relationships in any of the usual ways. Normal children, for example, differentiate their mothers from other adults very early on, and greet them by various signs long before speech proper is acquired. They tend to experience anxiety when separated from their mother, and seek comfort and enjoyment from her in cuddling. Similarly, a usual and developing form of contact with others is that of a meeting of glances from the eyes. In pre-school children it is normal that activities which seem to be purely centred on self-manipulation, the making of cries and unarticulated noises and so on characteristic of infants, diminish quite sharply with age, giving way to exploratory activities with objects, the environment, human and material, and to increasingly effective efforts at communication and contact with others.

In some children this process is arrested very early in childhood (before the thirtieth month) or does not develop. The most obvious sign is that such children do not learn to speak adequately or to respond to speech; they may be echolalic and make pronominal reversals if they speak at all; they make none or few eye contacts; they do not play in normally exploratory and constructive ways. They tend to develop ritualistic and compulsive movements or other similar phenomena. They seem completely turned inwards and out of contact with their material and human surroundings; they are sometimes hyperkinetic, sometimes withdrawn. They tend to test low in general ability and there is a marked discrepancy between non-verbal (which may be well above average) and verbal ability. Although they often give the impression of alertness, of an intelligence struggling to get through, many such children in the past have been considered simply as profoundly or severely intellectually retarded (as some of them are), or as examples of childhood schizophrenia or psychosis.

The basic difficulty which seems to underlie the problems presented by such children (and which differentiates them from the severely retarded or aphasic children whom they resemble) is found in an unusual weakness in language development arising from a central cognitive disorder in the processing of symbolic or sequenced information.[11] It seems likely that it is this which leads to their general difficulty of contact with mother and other adults and children, both by the impediment it places in the way of oral communication and by the responses their behaviour evokes.

In the present state of our knowledge (which is not great), such children (like many others) are probably best helped by being placed as early as possible in a good nursery school under the care of a teacher who can tolerate their oddities of behaviour, encourage contacts with others and gently insist upon communication. Older children apparently belonging to this group have been treated in special units, sometimes confined to the autistic and sometimes mixed with children having complementary handicaps, and having high staff/pupil ratios (varying from 1:1 to 1:4). In such circumstances, and especially with those children having initially tested I.Q.s above 44, about a quarter of autistic children show considerable improvement in emotional responsiveness, diminution of stereotypies, increased parallel and co-operative play, and improvement (where this is appropriate) in reading.

Many different remedial approaches have been tried based upon different rationales or theories: operant conditioning and forms of behaviour therapy; 'regressive therapy' based upon the assumption that the child has suffered an early trauma in relations and must be allowed to regress and start again; permissive remedial education; and a highly structured, directive Montessori type of remedial teaching. On the whole, it is the directive rather than the non-directive, the educational rather than the therapeutic, approaches which seem to have had most success.[12]

That the results are not, so far, very encouraging is probably for two reasons: the difficulty of adequate differential diagnosis between severe intellectual subnormality and a severe selective impairment in language communication and in the associated developmental social learning; and a lack of well-worked-out remedial strategies. However they are treated, autistic children, like severely subnormal or any other very handicapped children, raise very acute and chronic social and family problems with which parents need considerable and continuous help, not only to mitigate the effect of such a child on other children in the family, but to co-operate effectively in any remedial programme.

THE MILDLY INTELLECTUALLY RETARDED

Between children such as those just described and others whose intelligence' allows them more or less readily to profit by ordinary schooling, there is an even larger group, amounting to 2 or 3 per cent of the population[13] who, though capable of progress with specially adapted curricula, constitute a considerable social and educational problem, with which the ordinary teacher may not be equipped to deal, especially in a large class, unless special provision is made. For such children, whose ability level is between I.Q. 40 to 50[14] and I.Q. 60 to 70 (although I.Q. is not the unique criterion), special classes, schools or institutions have been set up in most European countries.[15] Unfortunately, however, by the very provision made for them, these pupils are often completely segregated from other children, sometimes wholly or partly from their parents,[16] and even from freely mixing in the community. Equally with the more profoundly subnormal, they are still often labelled mentally *defective*. In nearly half the cases no demonstrable physical or physiological pathology can be alleged as cause for their intellectual inferiority,[17] and in the present state of our knowledge many must be regarded merely as deviating below the average in ability in much the same way as highly able children deviate above the average—that is to say, they are *subnormal* and not defective. Such a distinction, though it may seem verbal, has important implications for the handling of such children. The very term 'defect' seems to imply medical treatment; whereas in most cases the main factor in helping such children to develop, even when they are otherwise handicapped, is a wisely adapted and optimistic special education for themselves, and a sound system of social and psychological help for their families. Some children, especially those with additional handicaps, or who are generally inferior physically, may have need of special medical supervision; a few must of necessity pass much of their time in hospitals or institutions. In some cases a genuine but milder inferiority of learning ability has been heavily compounded and aggravated by a home background which is unstimulating or disorganized.[18] All should benefit from some sort of specially adapted education, and for most this may be more conveniently given in special schools or classes attached to ordinary schools directly under the control of the education authorities. A closeness of integration with the ordinary education system and ease of transfer from special to normal classes is the more important, since cases occur of children who, while apparently irremediably and severely subnormal in their early life, improve in middle or in late childhood to the point where a return to the ordinary school is not only feasible but desirable.[19]

THE DULL-NORMAL[20]

Moderately and severely intellectually retarded children of the kinds just described, whose functional learning ability in general is less than, or barely equal to, two-thirds of the average, are relatively easily detected in the pre-school period or at least in their earlier primary school years, when they come into contact with their contemporaries under the care of a trained teacher. There remains a group, numerically some four or five times larger and amounting to at least some 8 to 10 per cent of the school population, for whom few European countries make any truly adequate provision. This group contains those who, intellectually speaking, function at a level some 15 to 40 per cent poorer than the average for their age. In terms of intelligence quotients on standardized individual tests, they range between 65 and 85–90. In the early stage of schooling, at least, their dullness may be apparent only when they are carefully observed. Many of them pass undetected throughout the whole compulsory schooling period, though they may be regarded by their teachers as passive, lazy, lethargic or merely 'culturally underprivileged'. They are slower to develop in almost everything: they often have speech defects; many of them have minor neurological, physical or health handicaps; they may learn to read later than the average, or acquire only the more mechanical aspects of reading, lagging markedly behind in comprehension; they experience especial difficulty in problem arithmetic, and at the secondary stage find the more abstract aspects of curricula beyond their grasp. The acquisition of adequate social attitudes and habits, particularly where these involve a foresight of consequences, may be slower and more difficult for them. As they go through school, even if they live up to their apparently limited ability (which in point of fact few of them do), they tend to become more and more backward compared with others of their own age.[21] Not infrequently they are dogged with the comment 'could do better' with its implication that only their laziness stands in the way of improvement. They tend to repeat classes and to drop out of the system as soon as they legally can.

This group is swollen by a variable number of others whose general functional ability, when tested on adequate individual tests, is in most respects within the normal range but whose work in school is clearly below their apparent capacity and who seem to be dull to their teachers. Sometimes these children in their early schooling have done reasonably well in things like arithmetic, which are almost exclusively taught by the school, but less well in reading or other verbal aspects of the curriculum because of a linguistic or cultural handicap. Sometimes their poor functioning is the result of emotional problems or continuing difficulties at home; sometimes they have a selective (and often undetected) neurological or sensory handicap or developmental disorder which directly affects their ability to profit from school. Most usually, both their capacity and motivation are limited largely by environmental influences. Many physically handicapped children fall into this group in terms of their functional capacity to learn—most of them for the reasons discussed later in this chapter.

VARIETY, MULTIPLICITY AND COMPLEXITY OF HANDICAP

It must not be assumed that the categories so far discussed are anything but arbitrary, or that the lines of demarcation between them can be accurately determined either in terms of intelligence quotient or of any other single criterion, or combination of criteria—educational, social or medical. In practice, at each of the notional borderlines there are many children who are assigned to one or the other category as much in terms of the availability and flexibility of the provision made as according to any fixed criterion.

We must, too, beware of the effect of labelling upon thinking and upon practice in the field of subnormality. For example, it used to be believed that the I.Q., properly determined, represented a stable, reliable and predictive measure which, for most children by and large, would remain the same throughout life and predict within fairly precise limits what the individual could achieve. Thus our labels were thought to be deterministic. There are, it is true, quite high correlations between I.Q. at say 6 or 7 and at 10 or 12 for groups of normal or subnormal children; and this seems to indicate stability. Quite apart, however, from the possibility that this might be a self-fulfilling prophecy (children tending to conform to the expectations based by parents and teachers on the initial measure) the correlations may conceal two quite separate but related phenomena. A high correlation would be obtained when the group remained in much the same order on the second test but when the general over-all performance of most individuals in the group had gone up or down. Thus the group could increase (or decrease) in ability relative to the population as a whole though remaining stable within itself. The second phenomenon is that of change in the status of individuals relative to the rest of the group. Correlations as high (and statistically significant) as 0.8 or 0.9 are compatible with changes in the I.Q. of some individuals by as much as 15 to 20 points or even more.[22] Thus, while an adequate measure of 'intelligence' or general ability to learn is an important part of any diagnostic procedure and, cautiously used, is valuable in setting *minimal* limits of expectation, it must not be taken, in any simplistic prognostic sense, to determine the maximum potential. Equally, any other measure of present performance—in reading, for example—is valuable for what it is rather than as a predictor of what could happen under really favourable circumstances.

We also know that there are many more children classified as subnormal or dull by educational criteria than there are adults who would be so classified. Probably this is because learning in school is more difficult than is the maintenance of one's adjustment later in some suitable social and vocational niche, and because adult life calls less upon some of the capacities crucial to formal school success.

Many children classified as intellectually retarded, and some at least of the dull, may in fact be genuinely and irremediably so, either for genetic or perinatal physiological reasons. Only rarely does anything like a truly dramatic upward change in general intellectual power occur. But the effective functioning of such children as adolescents and adults, their stock of useful knowledge and skills, their adjustment to life generally and to earning a living are highly dependent upon skilled and sensitive teaching, which takes an optimistic rather than a deterministic view of capacity. A far larger proportion of the dull and mildly retarded, much larger than most school systems have been ready to admit, function subnormally as a result of markedly adverse environmental

TABLE 1. Proportions of various grades of intellectual retardation among children of school age

Degree of [23] intellectual retardation	Terms in common use	Approximate I.Q.[24] levels and deviation (σ) below mean	Approximate [25] percentage in population of school age
Profoundly retarded ⎱	Idiot	below 20: $> -5{\cdot}3\sigma$	⎱
Severely retarded ⎰		21–35: $-5{\cdot}3\sigma$ to $-4{\cdot}3\sigma$	
Moderately retarded	Imbecile	36–50: $-4{\cdot}3\sigma$ to $-3{\cdot}3\sigma$	⎰ $2{\cdot}5 - 2{\cdot}6$
	Débile profond		
Mildly retarded	Feebleminded	51–70: $-3{\cdot}3\sigma$ to -2σ	
	Moron		
	Débile moyen		
Dull-normal	Dull and backward	70–85/90: -2σ to -1σ	10–15
	Peu doué—débile léger		
	Unterbegabt		
	Borderline mentally retarded		

factors, often occurring very early in life.[26] Many others, we suspect, function lower than is necessary either because of an undiagnosed disability or because steps were not taken early enough to palliate the effects of an apparently mild or even insignificant physical defect. Were we able to remedy such adverse early conditions in time, it seems likely that we could considerably reduce the numbers, even in the markedly subnormal group. Even when no attempt to remedy the lack of satisfactory and systematic intellectual stimulation can be made until such children enter primary school, some considerable improvement can be made in their general ability to learn, with sometimes an accompanying increase in I.Q. The hope of genuine cognitive improvement exists at any point in the life span.

CHILDREN WITH SENSORY HANDICAPS

THE BLIND AND THE DEAF

In common with severe mental handicap, but in contrast with many other groups, the distinctiveness of gross impairments of vision and hearing has been recognized in Europe for more than two centuries.[27]

The handicap of blindness is obvious to the layman, as is to a lesser extent the handicap of deafness, and marked cases of either are usually detected at an early age. Only comparatively recently have we come fully to appreciate the importance of sensory perception, particularly to cognitive development in infancy. Specific research into the intellectual, emotional and social problems posed by defects in the two major senses has begun to lead us to see that a child with a peripheral sensory defect is no different from any other child, except that his normal course of development is prejudiced by sensory defect, which leads to experiential deprivation unless development is safeguarded by educational means in the widest sense. The currently accepted aim of education for the sensorially handicapped is that they can and should be educated to take their place, as normally as possible, in the sighted and hearing world rather than be treated as a group apart destined to live in a closed and self-contained community of those similarly affected.

The psychology of the congenitally blind or deaf[28] and, to an extent dependent upon the age at which they become so, of those who become blind or deaf, may in many respects be regarded as one of frustration and particularly of early deprivation, a deviation in development caused by the reaction of potentially psychologically normal children to an environment made abnormal for them by their handicap. Hence, well-informed handling in infancy and in the pre-school period, and an education based upon the attempt to capitalize the child's resources and to find substitutes for the experiences (particularly in perception) of which he is deprived, may—unless there is more than peripheral damage—enable him very largely to develop a healthy and well-adjusted personality.[29] It would be foolish to contend that every blind or deaf child can become an adult who is socially, intellectually and economically as efficient as he or she could have been without a handicap; but a wise education can make the difference between a wholly or partially dependent, more or less maladjusted individual, and one who is a happy and effective human being within limits (albeit perhaps more specifically constraining) similar to those which are imposed on all of us by our differing temperamental and intellectual endowments.

Until comparatively recently, little attention has been given to the importance of the pre-school period in the subsequent development of the blind or deaf child; and, consequently, of the need for educational guidance and help to his parents from the earliest possible moment. Without such discriminating help very early in life, the blind child, for example, is likely to suffer in a number of ways. His blindness prevents him from those social experiences—smiles, games of 'peep-bo' and the like—which good mothering provides as a matter of course and which supplement and subsequently take the place of physical handling as assurances of love and as stimuli to development. Right from what Piaget calls the sensori-motor stage of the first months and years, he lacks the seeing element in the *gestalt* of visual-auditory-kinaesthetic perceptions which come from his exploration of his own body and of objects in his environment, and from play with adults and his own brothers and sisters. The essential foundation for his structure of concepts, the very basis of intelligence and the ability to learn, is lacking. His range of experience of objects is limited to those which come within the grasp of his hands, and perceptions of relationships in space are partially denied him, notably those leading to the basic concept of the permanence of the object. So too attitudes in his parents and others of over-protectiveness, excessive sympathy, covert or overt rejection or guilt, or even simply neglect, may early operate to colour his whole conception of himself and of society. Uninstructed, parents are not likely to appreciate or compensate for these and similar cumulative psychological deprivations and distortions produced by their child's blindness. It is small wonder that, by school age, many blind children seem to be retarded in their general cognitive, emotional and social development, are often markedly insecure, and have frequently developed a number of mannerisms and stereotyped movements, some at least of which are strikingly similar to those exhibited by children early deprived of maternal care and affection.

A child who is deaf may lack stimulus—intellectually and socially—in an even more serious way. Sound is important from birth or before, particularly the sound of a mother's voice, but up to the end of the first year of life concepts deriving from kinaesthetic and visual perception probably predominate in general development. Thereafter, and certainly from eighteen months onwards, hearing and speech begin to play an increasingly dominant part in the organization of the intellectual, social and emotional life. The child who cannot hear the speech of others, and cannot hear the sounds he himself makes, does not learn to speak unaided and may become mute. Lacking words, his conceptual growth is likely to be inhibited, delayed or turned awry[30] and his early social contacts are dependent exclusively on vision and touch. Such children often appear to be dull or even markedly subnormal; and are treated accordingly. To the negativism, which is a normal phase of the 2 to 3 year old, they may add a fiercely aggressive reaction to their frustrations and become tiresome problems. As in the case of the blind, the attitudes of parents and other adults, of older brothers and sisters, play a large—and sometimes seriously adverse—part in the deaf child's personal development.[31]

With a proportion of the blind and the deaf, difficulties of early development are complicated by associated motor or neurological disabilities or by the psychological consequences of prolonged or painful medical treatment. Others, because of their need for special care, because of the inadequacy of their homes or through the death or illness of their mother, pass at a very young age into institutions of one kind or another. Unless careful steps are taken to minimize the impact of such further complications on the child's already difficult growth task, the results may well be so far-reaching, even early in life, as to be virtually irreversible by subsequent educational or psychological handling.

Space does not permit a full treatment of the education of severely sensorially handicapped children, and the foregoing somewhat cursory and superficial analysis of the problems of the pre-school blind or deaf child has been made to draw attention to what is probably still the most neglected aspect in work for such children. Most European countries have well-developed school systems, and tried methods of teaching the blind and the deaf aged 5 and older. In the past half-century there has been a growing amount of research and practical experiment directed to the improvement of educational methods in this highly complex field, to a greater stress upon the general social and emotional development of such children, and to the training of specialized teachers aware of the problems involved. Yet it remains true to say that, as educators, we still do not recognize in any fully effective way the cardinal importance of those who take care of the child in the first three years of life. For want of the kind of help which parents need in understanding how to ensure the development of their handicapped child, and for want of places in nursery schools for such children from the ages of 2 or 3, much of the effort later put forth by the ordinary or special schools is frustrated. The work of the Ewings at Manchester, for example, has clearly demonstrated that, under expert guidance, parents can teach their deaf children to begin to speak and to comprehend speech through lip-reading from before the age of 2,[32] and that children thus taught will later come to school markedly advanced in their intellectual, social and linguistic development as compared with other deaf children. Similar research and controlled practical experiment are needed to improve the family education of the young blind child who is too often either left to the care of an uninstructed mother or prematurely removed to a residential nursery.[33] What is perhaps even more important is that, where careful efforts are made to prevent intellectual, emotional and social difficulties from arising and to compensate for the handicap on growth imposed by their disability, it becomes possible subsequently to educate a much higher proportion of blind or deaf children with other children in ordinary classes or in special groups or classes attached to the ordinary schools. This has been the growing experience in the United Kingdom. For example, whereas at the end of the nineteenth century virtually all deaf children receiving schooling in the United Kingdom were in special residential institutions, by 1971 only 10 per cent were being so educated, 20 per cent attended deaf schools as day pupils, 6 per cent attended schools for the partially hearing, 20 per cent attended units attached to ordinary schools and no less than 40 per cent were wearing hearing aids but were attending ordinary schools on their own with assistance from peripatetic and remedial teachers.[34]

THE PARTIALLY SIGHTED AND HARD-OF-HEARING CHILDREN

In many, if not most, European countries, the amount of provision for blind and for deaf children of school age is relatively sufficient, particularly since the numbers of the totally blind and deaf are diminishing with the control of certain diseases and an increase in our knowledge of intra-uterine and perinatal causes of these handicaps. The needs of partially sighted and hard-of-hearing children have not been met to the same extent and there are probably very many more cases than we at present think where the defect is extremely mild but its educational consequences disproportionately severe—particularly in relation to the early stages of learning to read. Even a moderately severe hearing loss of more than 30 decibels or a mild degree of short sight may not be detected prior to school entry, and not even then until a marked failure to learn to read draws attention to it. When the defect of vision or hearing is less than total but severe enough to attract attention in the school period, only too often it leads to children being grouped along with the totally blind or the deaf. The best current practice indicates that teachers, especially those concerned with very young children, should be trained to detect and bring forward for specialized examination likely cases of visual defect and auditory loss; that periodic screenings of the school population should be made, and that, partly through special classes, partly through the use of sight-saving apparatus or hearing aids, and partly through the adaptation of methods in ordinary classes, most of such children can be helped without resorting to segregated special treatment. Again, however, the emphasis must be placed on early detection prior to school entry and upon continued, specialized, psychological, educational and medical guidance for the child's family and for the school which receives him.

CHILDREN WITH SPEECH DEFECTS

Defects and deficiencies in speech are one of the commonest handicaps in children and are sometimes related to defects in hearing, though by no means always. Intelligible spoken language of considerable range and complexity has usually been acquired by normally developing children by the age of 4 or 5, although of course a number of infantile phonetic substitutions may persist, which disappear spontaneously in most cases by the age of 7. But among 7-year-old British children something between 10 and 13 per cent (more boys than girls and more difficulties among children from the lower socio-economic groups) still have an appreciable degree of speech impairment.[35]

As might be expected, the most important groups of children with language defects are the deaf and hard-of-hearing, the intellectually retarded and those with complex forms of brain damage. In addition, some with organic causes (for example, cleft palate) and many more for psychological and social reasons have enunciatory and emotional difficulties or marked developmental lags, which show themselves as lisping, lalling, stammering (1·1 per cent of 7 year olds)[36] and sometimes a determined mutism or marked lack of reaction. The causes are extremely complex and, from the point of view of treatment, certain broad distinctions as to the basic problems involved are essential. In many deaf children, for example, the difficulty may well be a purely peripheral one—the child cannot hear sound and, therefore, unaided cannot acquire speech. On the other hand, there are children whose hearing is to all intents and purposes intact, but the language difficulty seems to arise from a weakness in tactile and visual perception.[37] Such children have considerable difficulty with time relations and sequencing generally,[38] as do the deaf as a group, largely because sequence in time—'before', 'now', 'after'—is characteristic of auditory stimuli as distinct from the simultaneity of visual ones. There are, too, some children whose difficulties or deficiencies in speech seem to be relatively simple developmental lags which time and some therapeutic help will put right. There are others where the primary problem is psychological and emotional, demanding not so much remedial work on speech itself as help in personal development; yet others, where the difficulties are due, as much as anything, to an impoverished verbal-cultural background in early life.

Whatever its origin, a language difficulty of any sort, particularly if it is severe, presents considerable difficulties for a child, especially in school. For example, in a study of 215 7-year-old children[39] having defective speech but whose hearing was normal, it was found that 34 per cent were non-readers compared with 2·8 per cent of a normal control group; 32 per cent had little or no ability in number work (3·5 per cent of controls) and only 23 per cent (as compared with 64 per cent of controls) were rated by their teachers as 'stable'; and 47 per cent were considered 'maladjusted' (13 per cent of controls). Even when eighty-two children with recognized educational difficulties[40] were eliminated from the comparison with normals, there was still a much higher proportion in the speech-impaired group of children with difficulty in reading and calculating than in the general control group.

Certain other findings of this study also seem to be important educationally. There is, as well as the preponderance of boys (2:1), a correlation of speech defect with social class and birth order. Children from manual working-class groups were more likely to have speech defects, and later-born children were more likely to have difficulty. Many more of the speech-impaired than of the control group were children born pre-term, had impaired vision (three times as frequent), actual or latent squint (twice as frequent) and some degree of clumsiness (three times as common). Even of those not considered to be educationally subnormal, many more of the speech-defective children than of the controls showed marked weakness in such perceptual tests as 'draw a man' and 'cognitive-design'. Taken together, these data suggest that some of these children at least show not only a speech weakness but an all-round mild inferiority, coupled with a measure of social disadvantage which calls for sustained, positive educational support.

This study also underlines the importance, both in itself and as a symptom of more general vulnerability, of an even relatively mild speech and communication difficulty in a child. Speech is an essential intellectual instrument; and it is deeply and intricately connected with the whole social and emotional life. Thus, even though in some cases a speech defect may have a purely organic origin and be concerned uniquely with the conformation of the vocal organs, it very quickly acquires psychological meaning for the child and for his milieu. If neglected, it readily becomes the crystallizing point of a profound personality disturbance, as well as an educational handicap of the first magnitude. Speech defects—notably stammering and stuttering, lisping and some forms of mutism—are by no means always organic in their origin, but are the reflections of a disturbance in the whole emotional growth of the child. Early detection of any marked anomaly of speech and a careful physical, neurological and psychological examination which attempts to differentiate causes and effects are thus an essential basis for effective remedial action. Detection must in the main come from parents and teachers, who see the child in his daily life and have the oportunity of observing him or her in a variety of contexts. The examination and subsequent care of a child who is defective in speech is a matter for a team—composed of psychologist, audiometrist, otolaryngologist, paediatrician, speech therapist, social worker and the child's teacher—able to call at need upon even more specialized diagnostic and remedial skills.

A growing practice in Europe is to set up diagnostic and remedial speech clinics for such children and to provide a certain number of special classes for the worst cases. Unfortunately, where such clinics exist outside the education system or in the absence of adequate psychological services, speech therapy or surgical intervention is often unaccompanied by the attempt to readjust the child's emotional life and re-educate what is often an immature, disturbed or regressive personality. Frequently, too, where the speech-defective child attends an ordinary school and has to be absent from his class at regular intervals to attend the clinic, no attempt is made to see that he makes up what he has missed.[41] The remedy risks being worse in its consequences than the disability itself.

CHILDREN WHO SUFFER FROM CHRONIC PHYSICAL DISORDERS

THE DELICATE

Quite apart from congenital malformations of the limbs, there is a number of chronic diseases and disorders, many of them congenital, some with an onset in the early pre-school years and some supervening (or declining and disappearing) with the onset of puberty. Their prevalence is in general small and, in school-age children, relative to other handicaps, minimal, because many of them prove fatal in early life.[42] Some, like the streptococcal forms of rheumatic fever and juvenile rheumatoid arthritis, are somewhat in decline in the developed countries, although increasing with urbanization elsewhere; others are diseases, defects and malformations of major organs, particularly the heart, lungs and genito-urinary system, and in many cases respond to surgery; yet others are disorders of metabolism, like diabetes or phenylketonuria which, detected and treated in time, have little direct effect on development except that they may demand routine treatment and supervision.

In general, such physical disorders and defects constitute a problem for a child's development more because of their effects on family life, on the relations between the afflicted child and his mother, and because of the circumscription they may put on normal activity either necessarily (as, for example, with haemophiliacs) or because of parental over-protectiveness.

CHILDREN WITH ASTHMA

Two of such chronic disorders of rather different kinds and of a relatively high prevalence should be touched upon more especially. Of these, the first is asthma. Its prevalence, although considerable, seems to vary widely in different groups and countries. The figure given, for example, for Sweden is 1 per cent of the total population and for the United States 0·5 per cent,[43] and in both countries the percentages are higher for children of school age (between 2 per cent and 5 per cent).[44] One-third of the children in schools for the delicate in the United Kingdom are asthmatic.[45] Numerically, in fact, asthma seems to be seven or eight times more frequent than sensory handicaps, and six times more frequent than orthopaedic conditions.

Asthma, which is frequently connected with other allergic symptoms—for example infantile eczema—is in its severe form, though rarely fatal, a distressing and unpredictable illness. For the child who suffers the acute difficulty in breathing during an attack and for the parents who observe such an attack, it is a very disturbing or even frightening experience. One might well expect that it would have a considerable effect upon the child's emotional development and upon parental attitudes towards him, particularly in terms of the restrictions which they may feel obliged to impose. It has also been argued that asthma is itself a psychosomatic disease and psycho-analytic theories tracing it to fear of separation from an unconsciously rejecting but consciously protective mother have been put forward; but the research evidence does not support this view, nor the idea that mothers of asthmatics are more emotionally disturbed than mothers of other handicapped groups of children.[45] One further belief, that asthmatic children are highly intelligent and over-achievers in school, if it has not been entirely dispelled by research, has been called very much into question.[46] In general, asthmatic children do tend to do somewhat better on tests of intelligence than average, but this may, as much as anything, be because more of them come from middle-class homes, and because more such children tend to have sedentary hobbies. Similarly, their educational achievements—at least at age 11—do not differ from those of normal children[47] and when their reading attainment is compared with their level of general ability, it seems that more than twice as many as normal[48] are underachieving in reading. Indeed, one Belgian[49] study found that sixteen out of twenty severely asthmatic children were one to three years behind in their school work. It seems highly probable that the educational difficulties of many asthmatics stem from a much greater than average absence from school, and since there is some evidence of an association between *severe* asthma, large families and the semi- and unskilled socio-economic groups, those who miss most schooling are probably those least likely to receive help at home to make up for lost school work.[50]

EPILEPTIC CHILDREN

Epilepsy is a very different kind of disability and in some ways more frightening even than asthma. Because of its origin in the cerebral cortex, it is likely to have profound effects upon all aspects of the emotional and cognitive life, either directly by lowering impulse control, disturbing intellectual function and so on, or by the fears created in the child by his seizures, and the reactions of others to them. Usually, it seems, both aspects—the neurological and the psycho-social—interact. The disease itself is highly variable; from *petit mal*—a moment or two of unconsciousness—to the many different forms of *grand mal*; from cases where there is a marked and prolonged epileptic aura, with confused, aggressive, anti-social states, to others where seizures, although dramatic, may be few and far between, occur only at night, or in fact be almost completely controlled by medication. Finally, while *petit mal* may in many cases disappear after childhood, it may in some others change into *grand mal*. Only rarely does severe epilepsy become anything but worse with the stresses of puberty.

Its prevalence is even more difficult to estimate precisely than that of asthma—largely because it has many forms and causes and since epileptoid seizures may be symptomatic, for example, of cerebral tumours or occur as more or less isolated incidents of early childhood. The figures given by the World Health Organization (WHO) vary from 1·2 per 1,000 to 4 per 1,000 for children of school age; figures for Sweden suggest 1 per cent, and a study of a representative sample of 35,000 children from 5 to 15 in England suggested a figure of 7·5 per 1,000, of whom more than half had never been seen by a specialist.[51]

Popular belief has it that there is a definable epileptic personality, and for some, Julius Caesar (who had the 'falling sickness') and Napoleon Bonaparte are clear examples. However, it is difficult to know whether this is so, and whether any marked features of the personality of epileptics are directly associated with the disability or are the indirect results of anxiety and the attitudes of those around the growing child. With those, particularly, whose fits are controlled by drugs, there is some evidence of slowness of ideation, and perseveration. Some epileptics are marked by greater irritability and aggressiveness, changeability of mood and psychomotor instability. As might also be expected from the cerebral involvement, many severely and mildly intellectually retarded children are epileptic; but it is also true that some epileptics are of average or superior general ability. What is perhaps the most important factor is that the disease is still regarded as mysterious and shameful; and its manifestations are frightening to bystanders when they occur. Very often, for this reason, epileptics are excluded from ordinary school, or have schooling severely and frequently interrupted. Even sufferers from *petit mal*—which may go unnoticed in school—are liable to miss out essential steps because of a momentary loss of consciousness. Once sufferers have left school, and not only those who are mentally subnormal but even those of average or good general ability educated in ordinary classes, they may find their vocational possibilities severely restricted. This restriction may be reasonable (for example driving some kinds of machinery and mechanically propelled vehicles is obviously out of the question for them) but often the grounds are very dubious indeed. Only something like 5–10 per cent of epileptics present real danger to themselves or others; yet 17 per cent of a group followed up recently in France could not or would not work.[52]

MOTOR-HANDICAPPED CHILDREN

Another sizeable group, some sub-groups of which are declining in numbers, is that of the motor or orthopaedically handicapped. The prevalence of such crippling conditions in a population varies very considerably from time to time according to a wide variety of factors. For example, some years back many children suffered from poliomyelitis which left severe physical sequels; immunization has very greatly reduced this cause. More recently in some European countries, children with severe deformities and crippling were born as the result of the side effects of the drug thalidomide taken by mothers during pregnancy. At the present time, a most serious (and readily preventable) cause is accidents during childhood, especially in the home but also in traffic. Something around 4–5 children per 1,000 of school age in developed countries have marked orthopaedic anomalies. The figure may well be higher in developing countries, particularly since poliomyelitis, rare now in Europe, is on the increase elsewhere.

Most orthopaedically handicapped children are in other respects normal and the developmental problem is similar to that of many of the blind or the deaf—that of compensating for the depriving effects of their disability and preventing it from becoming a pervasive intellectual, emotional and social handicap because of the attitudes growing up around it.[53] With suitable equipment, all but a very few of such children can become mobile[54] quite young and later attend ordinary schools. Many more than at present could do so if buildings were slightly modified to meet their needs.

However, among children with motor impairments, there are two sizeable sub-groups whose handicaps tend to be associated with damage to the central nervous system—children with cerebral palsy and children with spina bifida. These groups, the second of which—spina bifida—is of increasing importance, illustrate the change which the past two or three decades have brought about in the developed countries. The 'simpler' forms of orthopaedic handicap supervening at birth or in infancy are becoming less frequent in developed countries, as are those related to poliomyelitis, tuberculosis, rheumatism and the like. On the other hand, many children, whose handicaps involve damage to the central nervous system and who had a low rate of survival in the past, can now not only survive but benefit greatly from early surgery and other forms of treatment. We are therefore confronted by an increasing proportion (and number) of children with very complex disabilities—physical and mental.

CEREBRALLY PALSIED CHILDREN

The most complex and varied group recognized for educational purposes is that of the so-called cerebrally palsied. Because of their often gross physical handicap and of their cognitive difficulties, many were treated in the past as low-grade mental defectives and others as simply 'crippled'. Their recognition as a very heterogeneous and complex group of handicapped and our understanding of the nature of their difficulties has only come about in the past two or three decades.

We now know that a number of children, as the result of intra-uterine degenerative and toxic factors,[55] natal cerebral haemorrhage, asphyxia and the like, suffer lesions of the cerebral cortex or of other parts of the brain which affect the innervation of the physical system and may selectively or generally impair intelligence. Such children frequently present the appearance both of deep mental defect and of severe physical handicap. Surveys in the 1950s suggested that the incidence of all types of cerebral palsy in the United

Kingdom was about 1 per 1,000 children from 0 to 16,[56] and that, of these, the principal types are spastic[57] (about 80 per cent) and athetoid[58] (10 per cent), and those showing ataxias, tremors, rigidities and mixed symptoms (about 10 per cent).

Any or all of the motor functions are likely to be affected to a greater or lesser degree: some cases show rigidity, flaccidity or athetosis of all four limbs, some those on one side or in lower limbs only. Many, especially among the athetoids, have difficulties in the innervation of the vocal organs such that they cannot learn, unaided, to speak; others have specific defects of hearing or vision. In some, the motor handicap is relatively small and the cognitive impairment profound; in others the motor impairment is very severe, but the cognitive level is normal or superior.

As we have said, the more severely affected were in the past often treated as idiots or imbeciles and for want of adequate physical and educational treatment became bedridden or institutionalized. A more careful examination of the group reveals, however, that, while the cerebral lesions or arrested development in many cases do affect intellectual development, and while rather more than half of all cerebrally palsied children are either mildly, moderately or severely intellectually retarded, there exists a considerable group which, under favourable conditions, can be educated to at least an average level and for whom, by physiotherapy, speech therapy and other forms of physical treatment, a great deal can be done. Nor is the educational or indeed vocational hopefulness of a case limited by the degree of crippling. The assessment of the child's future prospects is complicated and must be based upon a knowledge of the physical and social condition of the child, upon an estimate as accurate as possible of the mental level, and upon a careful qualitative analysis of intellectual functioning.[59] For no other group is the need for close understanding and team work between psychologist, specialized teacher, orthopaedic specialist, physiotherapist and speech therapist so clear—not only at the stage of initial examination, but continuously throughout childhood.[60] The demands of physical, educational and psychological handling often compete; for example, it may be thought necessary for the progress of physiotherapy that the child should be temporarily prevented from using his hand in a particular way, although this movement is almost his sole means of communication for educational purposes and to restrict him would have a devastating effect emotionally. It may be that some exhausting treatment is recommended just as the child has begun to master reading; or that physiotherapy or speech therapy are failing because of a psychological discontinuity or temperamental difficulty in the child himself which can be detected and explained only by the psychologist. In all such situations—and they abound in the education and training of cerebrally palsied children—a decision must be arrived at in terms of the whole development and needs of the individual and not in terms solely or predominantly of one speciality or form of treatment.

Attempts to educate such children have expanded rapidly in recent years but, owing to the amount and variety of equipment, the high staff ratio and the specialized accommodation required, they are expensive.[61] In the United

Kingdom, many centres exist where education and physical treatment are combined and where children who are fairly certain to profit from the expensive and complex services given are admitted. The most successful of these tend to be special day schools[62] to which children from a wide geographical area are brought by car and ambulance and where the facilities for education and for physical treatment are centralized. Such day provision has the advantage that direct and continuous contact is maintained with the home, and, by participating actively in the life of the school, the mothers and fathers are brought into partnership in the education and training of their child and can continue at home certain of the physical and educational activities necessary to progress. Similar provision is now made in most of the countries of Western Europe, Australia and North America.

SPINA BIFIDA

This is another congenital condition. If untreated in the immediate post-natal period, it results in hydrocephalus (abnormal head enlargement) and probable consequent brain damage. It is a malformation of the spine, visible at the moment of birth as a protruding sac usually covered only by a thin membrane and containing cerebro-spinal fluid. In the milder cases, this can be treated by surgical closure and seldom gives rise to problems; but if the swelling contains a malformed part of the spinal cord, there is danger of further damage and surgical closure has to be undertaken within a few hours of birth. Arising from the back lesion and disorder of the spinal cord, are likely to be paralysis of the lower limbs, abnormalities of bladder function, incontinence and, later on, limitation of sexual function. It is in these more serious cases that the danger of hydrocephalus with brain damage arises due to the obstruction of the flow of cerebrospinal fluid. In the past, few such children survived infancy and even among those who escaped hydrocephaly, 62 per cent had some mental handicap. Advances in surgery and medical care have increased the survival rate to about half and diminished the extent of brain damage; but, although nearly half of such children now survive beyond the age of 2, the survivors tend to have severe and complex physical disabilities, which put great demands on their families and on the medical, social and educational services. Spina bifida is now one of the major disabling congenital conditions among children, with a prevalence of about 3 per 1,000 births.[63]

Those who are hydrocephalic, apart altogether from any lowering of general ability, tend to have anomalies of cognitive function very similar to those found in cerebral palsy. Their eye–hand co-ordination may be poorer than average; they may have weaknesses in visual–spatial perception; special difficulty in figure–ground discrimination; and specific impairment in the perception of tactile stimuli—all aspects of cognition which would considerably add to the difficulties of learning, particularly learning to read.[64]

For the serious cases, repeated operations at a young age are common. For example, of seventy-four such children studied in Scotland,[65] twelve had had three operations, fifteen between seven and nine operations, and six had had more than ten—including a child of 5 who had had at least fourteen. Nor are operations confined to the early years; orthopaedic operations tend to interrupt primary and secondary schooling and for lengthy periods.

About a third of the children studied (32·4 per cent) in the Scottish sample had become fully independent in their mobility with aids, and a further 34 per cent using callipers and hand-aids were reasonably so. Less than a quarter needed no items of equipment, while more than a third needed three items of special equipment or more.

About one-third of these severely handicapped children attended ordinary schools, and many of them had done so from the nursery stage onwards; another quarter attended special day schools; 15·7 per cent had had no schooling. However, 41 per cent of those who did attend school had had a delay in entering or had been excluded from primary schooling for at least a year; many others had had long absences. The reasons for these absences, apart from hospitalization, are bowel or bladder incontinence, a mental unreadiness for schooling and in some cases the unsuitability of the facilities, making it difficult for staff to cope with the child.

One other feature of spina bifida is brought out by Woodburn[66] and seems to be characteristic of other multiply handicapped groups. The condition makes formidable demands on parents, and no matter what external help they get, some mothers and fathers have to spend hours every day in coping with appliances of various kinds, and devote a great deal of money and energy to travel. They may face distressing comments from others. Certainly the whole fabric of family life is deeply affected.

One might expect families to be disrupted and disintegrated by such strains, but the evidence—for spina bifida, for cerebral palsy and for thalidomide children's families—seems to be the other way. Indeed, there are signs that the family may become *too* cohesive, too intensely involved with the handicap—to such a degree that parents and siblings are seen not as individuals with their own rights but as existing only to serve the handicapped member. Paradoxically, such families are likely to get the approval of society because they are so devoted, whereas a better balance of interests might be more healthy for all concerned, and particularly for the handicapped member.

LABELLING

Throughout this discussion of the principal groups of handicapped children, we have been led into an inevitable and somewhat dangerous simplification, based upon two very highly questionable assumptions. The first is that the mainly medical diagnostic labels—sensory defect, orthopaedic handicap, mental defect or subnormality, and so on—are themselves reasonably precise and exclusive and suitable for categorizing children for administrative purposes and for estimating prevalences. The second, which is less overt but more damaging in its consequences for action if we are not fully aware of it, is that these diagnostic labels or categories have a necessary relation to the possibility of remedial physical treatment or to the likelihood of favourable psychological and educational development.

The fact of the matter is that most of the categories which are used are as much determined by the particular viewpoint of the specialist using them as they are by the causal nature of the symptoms on which they are based. They tend to masquerade as diagnoses when in fact they are descriptions or labels attached to a salient feature. It is probably as much for this as for any other reason that estimates of prevalence of any condition vary from country to country and from one study to another—particularly where the category concerned (like for example 'autism') covers an ill-understood condition, or where (as for example 'cerebral palsy' or 'epilepsy') there are great differences in kind, origin and severity of the symptoms.

Labels of medical origin and medical diagnostic categories imply the use of the disease model—a pathological condition coupled with a physical remedy. This is, of course, often appropriate to the physical aspects of handicap; but, as we have seen, there is no direct or linear relationship between physical condition and psychological or educational consequences and remedies. If such a relationship is assumed, openly or tacitly, it can easily result in a deterministic attitude to what can be done to enable a child to develop satisfactorily in spite of his disability.

Labelling tends to have another consequence. Labels tend, in the eyes of parents, of children themselves, and even in those of the professions concerned, to acquire meanings of their own and a mythology which causes labelled individuals to be included in some categories of treatment and excluded from others.[67] Moreover, fashions change and a label may by its fashionableness attract wrong diagnoses or be sought after by parents anxious to get the best treatment for their child—or anxious to avoid the guilt or blame or social stigma they believe is attached to some other label. Pressure from a few parents, armed with a fashionable but ill-understood diagnosis, may lead to the setting up of special facilities which, in themselves not strictly necessary, deprive other larger groups of resources.

THE MULTIPLICITY OF HANDICAP

The whole area is rendered more difficult by the fact that handicap is rarely simple. There are, of course, cases where there is a single disability without other complications. But the more closely we study most children held to be handicapped, the more we come to realize that very many of them indeed have some added difficulty, either associated with their handicap in some sort of direct way and on a physical level, or acquired because their handicap has distorted their growth. Few physically handicapped children escape some measure of learning difficulty and in some this is sufficiently severe to lead to a general dulling of the power to learn; they appear to be—and very often are functionally—intellectually subnormal.[68]

This is a circumstance which throws some additional doubt upon the wisdom of labelling according even to the main presenting handicap. It also raises problems of specialist supervision and of too highly specialized training for teachers, who may find themselves teaching (and trained to teach) blind children for example, few of whom will be without an additional handicap of another kind, perhaps of equal or greater educational importance than blindness.

Usually such children are classified for administrative and educational purposes in terms of what is thought to be the major difficulty. Thus, a mildly mentally retarded or physically handicapped child who is blind will probably be educated as a blind child rather than be put with mentally subnormal or orthopaedic cases, although within blind education there may be segregation according to ability. Similarly, most children with cerebral palsy, which is often accompanied by crippling, by defects of vision, hearing and speech, as well as by anomalies in intellectual growth, are likely to be distinguished from other orthopaedically handicapped and be placed in a school or class staffed by those specially acquainted with the problems of cerebral palsy. In many cases—and certainly for those for whom integration in ordinary schools is impracticable—this may be the best that can be done. What is important, however, is to recognize that the principal problem with all handicapped children is likely to be a learning one imposed by the handicaps present in the child. In its turn this means that the teacher (and the psychological and medical consultants) should be aware of the effects of other handicaps—particularly of intellectual retardation, difficulties in speech, or in sensory perception—and be helped to deal with them as well as with the deafness, blindness or other major physical handicap.

There exists a hard core of cases in which there are at least two gross physical or sensory handicaps, and it is difficult to say which is paramount in educational importance. An extreme example, of course, is the blind-deaf child, who needs the help of specialized techniques derived both from work with the blind and from work with the deaf. In general, too, the cerebrally palsied child tends to have more than one gross handicap. Fortunately, relative to the numbers of the much less complicated cases of blindness, deafness, subnormality or crippling, such very extreme and difficult cases of multiple handicap are few. In the past many children suffering from them have been considered ineducable, and even now one meets cases of children who have been passed as failures from one specialized school to the next, before being finally excluded from the education system entirely, to pass their lives either in hospital or an asylum or as a burden upon their family.

But multiple handicap is by no means confined to such relatively small groups of cases. As was pointed out in the discussion of intellectual subnormality, many children whose main difficulty seems to be a slowness of cognitive development are in fact suffering from 'minor' physical, sensory or neurological handicaps as well, and a considerable group must be regarded as disadvantaged in the sense that a main contributory cause of their learning difficulties is a disorganized or deprived early environment. Some will be found to have an accumulation of disabilities, no one of which seems in itself to be severe enough to be predominant in causation but which, in combination, amount to a very formidable impediment to development in almost every field.

This is likely to be true particularly among the severely and moderately subnormal, but there are considerable proportions of the mildly subnormal and the dull who are similarly multiply handicapped. There are pupils with more or less severe degrees of emotional disturbance who, because of their difficulties, are unable to concentrate, or are turned in upon themselves, unwilling or unable to speak, and who are severely retarded in their academic and social development. Others, because of a marked instability or because of an abnormal lethargy, are unable to achieve more than a fraction of what their endowment should enable them to achieve. Another large group will be found to be merely severely educationally backward, often as the accumulated result of periodic absences from school or because demands for help made on them at home are too great, or—as is increasingly the case—they come from immigrant or migrant families. There will be those who have specific cognitive difficulties—difficulties, for example, in the visual organization of space or in the auditory analysis of sound—which impede or indeed prevent learning to read by conventional methods; others have a marked lack of development of cerebral dominance; or speech, visual or auditory defects[69] of a kind which escape all but the most competent psychological, physical or neurological diagnosis and which slow up or even prevent learning. A proportion, because of cerebral damage at or before birth, may present the appearance of a low-grade defect, have severe motor disturbance, spasticity or athetosis and many associated troubles, but yet have an intellectual capacity markedly above the average. In a few cases, where highly specific difficulties in reading or in arithmetic exist and cumulatively hamper general educational progress, one may suspect a neurodevelopmental lag or the existence of cerebral lesions undetectable as yet by neurological examination but which can be explored by suitable psychological tests of perception. Some of these children are hyperactive or markedly clumsy.[70]

It is this variety of capacity and of difficulty that makes imperative a careful examination of any child, whether overtly physically or sensorially handicapped or not, who is thought to be cognitively subnormal, or found to be failing to learn. His life history, and particularly that of his speech and general development, his social circumstances and family background must be studied; a careful series of paediatric and neurological examinations may have to be made, going well beyond the broad assessment of specific handicap; and certainly a thorough psychological examination must be carried out, not so much to forecast some future potentiality as to devise a specific programme of education at home and at school which will build upon what he can do. It is only on such a basis—which implies close team work among psychologist, social worker, medical specialist and, for children of school age, the teacher—that a real appraisal of potentialities and handicaps can be made, and the vital distinction be drawn between physical impairments, which may be palliated but cannot be removed, and the consequential handicap to development, which may be avoided or improved by the appropriate remedial action. Such appraisals should, of course, be provisional and, throughout the school period at all events, be subject to periodic and unprejudiced review,[71] based as much as anything upon the trained day-to-day observation of those who teach the handicapped child.

Similarity of apparently causal type of subnormality or similarity of present level of intellectual functioning do not necessarily imply similarity of educational treatment or of likely outcomes; and in this respect psychiatric labels and intelligence quotients continue, as we have stressed, to be misleading, especially when they become the basis of rigid administrative or legal classifications. The very complexity of handicapping conditions, the very differences in each child's circumstances, in his prospects of development, and the uncertainty of prediction of the way in which the interplay of temperamental, motivational and social factors with intellectual ability will operate, should lead to discriminating psychological examination, to sensitive, continued supervision and to a rich variety of educational provision.[72]

NOTES

1. For example mongolism (one chromosome too many), amaurotic family idiocy, etc.
2. For example antenatal effects of drugs on the foetus, or of disease processes such as maternal rubella.
3. For example cerebral damage due to damage at or shortly after birth.
4. Something can, however, be done by genetic counselling to discourage the birth of some types of children or to prevent the ill-effects of conditions in the mother. See: Carter, C. O. *Genetic counselling*.
5. Considerable research is at present under way to assess the effectiveness of techniques of operant conditioning with such children.
6. Even as early as 1954 (World Health Organization. *The mentally subnormal child*. Geneva, 1954 Technical report series, no. 75) the recommendation was made that all such children should be the responsibility of the education authorities. It was not until 1970 that this was implemented in the United Kingdom with important consequences for the training of staff as specialized teachers for such deeply handicapped children. *The last to come in* (London, Department of Education and Science. *Reports on education*, March 1971, no. 69) states that there are (in England and Wales) some 24,000 children in 330 training centres, 8,000 in hospitals and 750 in special care units. Until recently, such children had to be 'certified' and were passed over to the health authorities. If trained at all, those who cared for them had considerably less preparation for their work than did qualified teachers. The change of responsibility for their care and education recognizes that 'educational subnormality' is a continuum, that at all levels children are educable to some degree and require skilled teachers and that, since some children improve dramatically, movement from one group, class or school to another should be easy and not involve cumbersome rituals of decertification.
7. Hamerton, J. L. *Human cytogenetics*. New York, Academic Press, 1971, cited by Frizal, J.; Feingold, J. Génétique. *In*: Mande, R.; Masse, N.; Manciaux, M., op. cit., note 8, chapter 1, see also below note 13. In Tizard's inquiry (see following note 8) 80 per cent of the mothers of mongols were aged over 30 and 40 per cent over 40.
8. See: Tizard, J.; Grad, J. C. *The mentally handicapped and their families*. London, O.U.P., 1961.
9. Hermelin, B.; O'Connor, N. *Psychological experiments with autistic children*. Oxford, Pergamon, 1970.
10. The syndrome was originally described by Kanner in 1943 (Autistic disturbance of affective contact. *In: Nervous child*, 19/iv vol. 2, p. 217). A most exhaustive account of this group is given in Wing, J. K., ed. *Early childhood autism*. London, Pergamon, 1963.

See also: Bettleheim, B. *The empty fortress: infantile autism and the birth of the self.* New York, Free Press, 1967. Des Lauriers, A. M.; Carlson, C. F. *Your child is asleep: early infantile autism.* Homewood, Ill., Dorsey, 1969. Perhaps the best statement of knowledge to date is in Rutter, M. ed. *Infantile autism: concepts, characteristics and treatment.* London. Churchill Livingstone, 1971.

11. See: Rutter, M.; Bartak, L.; Newman, S. Autism: a central disorder of cognition and language. *In*: Rutter, M., ed. op. cit., see preceding note 10.

12. See: Rutter, M., ed., op. cit., see above note 10. Paper by Bartak, L.; Rutter, M. *Educational treatment of autistic children.* Only Bettleheim (op. cit., note 10) claims a success rate higher than 28 per cent. He states that 80 per cent of his forty patients had a fair or good outcome.

13. Estimates vary from country to country, in part because of differences of definition and in part because of the methods used in case-finding. The figure for profound, severe, moderate and mild retardation found in the Isle of Wight study cited in Chapter 1, note 2, is 2·6 per cent, of whom at least 2 per cent have I.Q.s above 50. However, other estimates, using different criteria and differing case-finding techniques, are lower. For example, F. M. Sorel (Les fréquences de la débilité mentale à Amsterdam dans les catégories d'âge de 10 à 13 ans. *In: Seminaire sur les enfants atteints d'insuffisance mentale.* Paris, Centre international de l'enfance, 1971) proposes combined criteria of adaptation to social demands (Vineland scale)—I.Q. lower than 80 (Wechsler Individual Scale for Children—WISC) and an onset in early childhood. By this, he calculates a prevalence of 1·8 per cent. However, by the strictly intellectual criterion, the figure is 2·37 (below I.Q. 80) or 1·69 per cent (below I.Q. 70). A French estimate (Hatton, F. et al. Etude sur les enfants suspects d'insuffisance mentale dans le département de la Haute Vienne. *In: Séminaire sur les enfants atteints d'insuffisance mentale.* op. cit.) gives a prevalence of 2·6 per cent below I.Q. 70, 4·4 per cent below I.Q. 80 (1·8 per cent between I.Q. 50 and I.Q. 70 and 1·8 per cent between I.Q. 70 and I.Q. 80). In the fourth French five-year plan (cited by Manciaux, M. Déficiences et maladies chroniques et prolongées: problèmes généraux. *In*: Mande, R.; Masse, N.; Manciaux, M. op. cit., note 8, chapter 1) the figures are 2·38 per cent for profoundly, severely and moderately retarded (*arriération mentale profonde*, 0·05 per cent; *arriération mentale sévère* 0·75 per cent; *arriération mentale modérée*, 1·35 per cent) and for the mildly retarded 4·4 per cent (*arriération mentale légère*—probably at least some of the dull in the present classification).

14. Children below I.Q. 50 are regarded as profoundly or severely retarded. They may be labelled as 'idiot' or 'imbecile' and are still excluded in some countries from the education system proper. The implied distinction is highly artificial. See note 6 to this chapter.

15. The provision in Belgium is fairly typical of Europe in general. There are special schools, most often day schools, boarding schools being reserved for those children whose families cannot accept them. In the province of Hainault, in agreement with the trade unions and organizations of artisans and shopkeepers concerned, schooling is completed by special vocational training for jobs in such industries as building, horticulture or farming. For those who cannot work in an open situation, sheltered workshops are supported by the state. In Holland every town and most of the large villages have at least one special school provided by the state for children with I.Q.s under 80. A similar situation exists in the United Kingdom, where about 1 per cent of children of school age are judged to need special schools or special class provision, although considerably fewer are actually being educated in such a way. In the canton of Geneva there are twenty-eight urban and two rural special classes. In France, for children between I.Q. 60 and I.Q. 87, there are some 1,300 special day classes, including 150 in the Paris region, with a total attendance of about 20,000. One thousand children are catered for in day centres which combine educational or vocational training with medical care. A further 10,000 children are cared for in residential, custodial establishments and psychiatric hospitals, and 7,000 in medico-pedagogic institutions. Between 1966 and 1970 the number of children in some form of special education in France more than doubled, as did the number of specialized institutions (Manciaux, op. cit., see above note 13). The situation in France is described by Pettit, J., et al., eds. *Les enfants et les adolescents inadaptés et l'éducation nationale.* Paris, Bourrelier, 1966. See also: World Health Organization. *Organization of services for the mentally retarded.* Geneva, 1968. Technical report series, no. 392.

For an enlightened discussion of the occupational and social problems of adult mental retardation, see: O'Connor, N.; Tizard, J. *The social problem of mental deficiency*. London, Pergamon, 1956; and for a more recent field study: Bayley, M. *Mental handicap and community care*. London, Routledge & Kegan Paul, 1973.

16. For example, an inquiry reported by the French Centre for Child Welfare to the International Child Welfare Congress at Zagreb, 1954, reported that, of thirty-three institutions for the mentally subnormal, seven had no contact with the family. Of thirty-one medico-pedagogic institutions in the Paris region, thirteen permitted visits on a fixed day once a month, ten on a fixed day several times a month, two when it suited the families, one had 'no rules', and one allowed visits in certain cases only; seventeen allowed children to go home during the holidays: two on exceptional occasions, five regularly but for short stays, ten for the whole of the school holidays. This was fairly typical in Europe, but in the past twenty years there has been considerable improvement in access in most countries, including, of course, France. Even so, the siting of many institutions in remote places and a persistence of custodial attitudes still inhibit full contact in many cases.

17. Many of them do, however, have additional handicaps (hearing loss, speech difficulty, motor impairment, visual defects and poor general physical condition). Of the educationally subnormal population studied by Williams and Gruber (*Response to special schooling*. London, Longman, 1968), 63 per cent had one or more handicaps additional to a low functional ability. Probably birth damage, speech defect and motor impairment are the three characteristics indicating possible neurological damage which are most closely causally associated with severe learning difficulty.

18. See the first volume of this series, *Constructive education for children* (London, Harrap; Paris, Unesco, 1975), especially chapter 6, p. 91–7, and chapter 9.

19. When populations in special schools for the intellectually retarded are examined, it is customary to find among them some children who, in terms of I.Q., are well above the borderline of I.Q. 70 or even I.Q. 80—for example, 11 per cent of the children in special schools in the French inquiry cited in note 16 were above I.Q. 80 but found themselves labelled as subnormal, largely because of severe learning difficulties and educational failure but also because of severe difficulties in their family backgrounds. Similarly in 1956, 34 per cent of children in schools for the educationally subnormal (ESN) in England had I.Q.s above 70 and 4·5 per cent above 80. From 1956 to 1959, the proportion of pupils with I.Q.s of 80+ rose from 7·5 per cent to 10 per cent in rural ESN schools. (United Kingdom. Ministry of Education. *Health of the school child, 1960–61*. London, HMSO, 1962.) This appears to indicate that a functional educational criterion is being used for placement rather than, or in addition to, ascertained intellectual retardation. The distinction is important since the outlook for children of different kinds may be very different. Williams and Gruber (*Response to special schooling*. London, Longman, 1968) found that children who left schools for the educationally subnormal and entered those provided for the severely retarded were distinguished from a second group who were able to enter ordinary schools. The first group was, in general, more evidently damaged as individuals—i.e. there was evidence of organic or neurological handicap ascertained early in life—whereas the second group contained those whose learning difficulties were more obviously attributable to a damaged family environment.

20. A briefer treatment of this group in relation particularly to school failure is given in the first volume in this series, *Constructive education for children*, chapter 11.

21. A recent survey by the Department of Education and Science (United Kingdom) (*Slow learners in secondary schools*. London, HMSO, 1971) showed that at least 14 per cent of all pupils in such schools were considered by the headmasters to require special treatment because of their backwardness. Such children suffer most at transition periods, particularly from the relatively small junior school to the larger secondary one. The crucial need was for specially trained teachers to conduct remedial and slow learning groups at the secondary stage.

22. Clarke, A. D. B.; Clarke, A. M. Consistency and variability in the growth of human characteristics. *In*: Wall, W. D.; Varma, V. P., eds. *Advances in educational psychology: I.*

London, University of London Press, 1972. In general, the Clarkes state, the worse the background the better the ultimate progress, often including substantial I.Q. increases between 15 and 30 points. See also Zazzo, R. *Les débilités mentales*. Paris, Armand Colin, 1969.

23. The first four categories are those recommended by the fifth WHO Seminar on Psychiatric Diagnosis, Classification and Statistics (Washington, 1969) for inclusion in the International Classification of Diseases (ICD). The fifth category is educationally of considerable importance and was included by the WHO Expert Committee in *The organization of services for the mentally retarded*. Geneva, WHO, 1968. Technical report series, no. 392. The Washington seminar on classification rejected it on the grounds that its inclusion would bring 16 per cent of the population into the general category of retardation. (See: Classification of mental retardation. Supplement to *Am. j. psychiatr.* (Washington, American Psychiatric Association), vol. 128, no. 11, May 1972.)

24. I.Q. scores are extremely useful. They give a sample of an individual's current level of functioning within standardized situations. But they should only be used when derived from professionally administered individual tests—and even then not in isolation—to determine a child's future. Reliance on such scales as the original Binet and its variants in estimating intellectual capacity can be criticized mainly on the grounds of their verbal-educational content and their inapplicability to populations very different in kind from the original standardization sample. Current practice includes non-verbal scales in the assessment of ability, and, in cases where assessment of cognitive function is critical, analytic tests of specific aspects of functioning are also used. It can, of course, be validly argued that, for children of school age, the verbal-educational content of the Binet derivatives, or better still of scales such as the Wechsler, is in itself a measure of some aspects of a child's prior learning and therefore an essential element in an examination concerned with educability and educational guidance. From the educational point of view, it is less sound to give weight to social and emotional factors at this stage (as is often done) and to allow these to determine in borderline cases. The result of such practices may be to turn the special school or class into a dumping ground for backward and disturbed children: those who do not necessarily have truly subnormal intellectual endowment but who, because of their emotional or social difficulties, are a nuisance in the ordinary class and should benefit from a different provision. This is not to say that social and emotional factors should be disregarded. A stable child of relatively low I.Q.—say 65—can, with the help of his parents and teacher, hold his own in a class for the dull and backward or even in an ordinary class, whereas an unstable or very disturbed one with an I.Q. of say 75 or 80 might be better off, at least for a time, in a special school or class. Placement in all borderline cases should be made on the basis of a careful case study and in terms of a knowledge of the school, class or even teacher proposed, rather than of rigid classifications by any kind of criteria. If differentiation of provision is to achieve its end, it must be matched by careful appraisal of the educable capacity of the child and of the circumstances which will best bring it forth.

In the case of populations in which the social and cultural conditions are quite different from those of the populations on which the test instrument was standardized, I.Q.s are likely to be grossly misleading. (See: 'Resolution on psycho-technical tests' of the Educational, Scientific, Cultural and Health Commission of the Organization of African Unity (Addis Ababa, 4 July 1969), cited in the American Psychiatric Association's supplement mentioned in note 23.)

It is for this reason, among others, that approximate limits in terms of a normal distribution in a *given population* are indicated in Table 1 in sigma units (σ) below the population mean; $\pm 1\sigma$ around the mean of a given population would include two-thirds of the population.

25. These percentages are approximations only, although the figure of 2·5 per cent for the retarded seems to be fairly stable in developed countries (but see note 13 in this chapter). However, I.Q.s above 50 tend to be correlated with social class and with cultural and economic conditions, and much dullness seems to be an accompaniment of poverty. Hence, even the large category of the mildly retarded who make up four-fifths of the whole retarded group might considerably fluctuate in prevalence according to changes in the general

conditions in which young children are brought up and educated as, *a fortiori*, would the dull-normal.

26. It should be noted that our increased knowledge of the way the ability to learn grows, and is structured by the environment, has led us to the idea that the low abilities of many children are the result of an upbringing which does not help them to develop the kinds of cognitive structures presupposed by our societies and especially by schools (see the first volume of this series, *Constructive education for children*, chapter six, p. 91 ff.). They form part of the 'subcultural group' of Lewis (see: Penrose, L. S. *The biology of mental defect*. New York, Grune & Stratton, 1949, p. 45) and remarked by C. Burt (*The backward child*. London, U.L.P., 1937) as being associated, in its prevalence, with the poorest sectors of big cities. More recently they have been seen as the target for 'compensatory education'. (See the first volume in this series, chapter nine, p. 177 ff.)

27. Preoccupation with the care and protection of the blind and of the blinded is, of course, much older, and many occupations (begging, professional mourning, soothsaying, handmill grinding, music, etc.) were entirely or partially reserved for them in some countries of the ancient world. Many of the blind made efforts, not only to acquire culture themselves, but to educate fellow-sufferers, e.g. Didymus of Alexandria (fourth century A.D.) who taught with a carved wooden alphabet. The first school for the blind seems to have been established by Haüy (1745–1822) in France and was followed by that founded in Liverpool (United Kingdom) in 1790. Developments elsewhere in Europe followed within two decades. The education of the deaf preceded that of the blind by several centuries. It seems to be agreed that the first great teacher of the deaf was the Spanish Benedictine monk Pedro Ponce de Leon (1520–84) and it was two Spaniards (Bolet of Madrid and Ramires de Carrion) who in the seventeenth century published the earliest textbooks on the education of the deaf. From Spain the inspiration came (through Kenelm Digby) to England and (through Jacob Perière) to France. Towards the end of the eighteenth century schools of considerable size were established in France (Abbé de l'Epée), Germany (Samuel Heinicke), and Britain (Thomas Braidwood). See: Frampton, M. E.; Rowell, H. G., eds. *The education of the handicapped*. Vol. I. London, Harrap, 1939; Pritchard, D. G. *Education and the handicapped*. London, Routledge & Kegan Paul, 1963, especially chapters 1–5.

28. Definitions of 'total' blindness and 'total' deafness vary from country to country and tend to differ according to whether one is concerned with educating the child, applying some form of disability allowance or placing him in employment. Both handicaps have tended to decrease in recent years because of better perinatal care, increased knowledge of the effect, for example, of streptomycin and the causes of retrolental fibroplasia. It seems that the deaf and partially hearing constitute rather more than 1 per 1,000 of the school-age population, and the blind and partially sighted nearly 2 per 1,000. In developing countries the incidence would be expected to be much higher.

29. For a fuller treatment of this topic see: Wall, W. D. The psychology of the handicapped child in relation to his family. *In: Child welfare in relation to the family*. Geneva, International Union for Child Welfare, 1955, p. 65–79.

30. There may be, perhaps, even with the partially hearing, a depression in the verbal conceptual area with associated weaknesses in reading and arithmetic, represented by as much as 21 points on the WISC verbal scale, as compared with a normal distribution of non-verbal ability. Hine, W. D. The abilities of partially hearing children. *Br. j. educ. psychol.* (Edinburgh), vol. 40, pt. 3, June 1970, p. 171–8.

Another study suggests that even a moderate bilateral hearing loss in 7-year-old children (35–54 dB on at least two speech frequencies) is associated with more poor speakers, poor readers, more children poor at number work and more who are not good at oral work, than in a control group of normal children. There were, too, more who were inferior in visual-spatial ability as shown by the Goodenough 'draw a man' test, but little evidence at this stage of more emotionally disturbed children. Many (15 per cent) of them also had vision of 6/12 or worse in the better eye, as compared with the controls (3·4 per cent). More of the children with severe *unilateral* hearing loss (55 dB or worse in one ear and normal hearing in the other) were rated as having poor speech, poor reading and poor oral ability than the moderately bilateral. Many more of these children (30 per cent as compared with 13 per cent of controls) were rated as maladjusted. Those children who had severe *bilateral* hearing loss (55 dB or more in both ears) had higher proportions than the other groups of those with poor reading, poor number work, poor oral work, poor muscular co-ordination and maladjustment. However, in all these groups it must also be remembered that half or more of the children were rated by their teachers as making satisfactory or above-average progress in reading, number and oral work. Peckham, C.; Sheridan, M.; Butler, N. School attainment of seven-year-old children with hearing difficulties. *Dev. med. & child neurol.* (London), vol. 14, no. 2, 1972.

31. D. M. C. Dale (*Deaf children at home and at school*. London, U.L.P., 1967) indicates the principal dangers and difficulties and ways of avoiding or minimizing them. See also: Watson, T. J. *The education of hearing-handicapped children*. London, U.L.P., 1966; Frère Donatien, et al. *Initiation de l'enfant sourd au langage*. Paris, Ed. sociales françaises, 1965; Charpentier, M. *L'épanouissement de l'enfant sourd en scolarité normale*. Paris, Ed. sociales françaises, 1966.

32. Ewing, I. R.; Ewing, A. W. G. *Opportunity and the deaf child*. London, U.L.P., 1947; *The handicap of deafness*. London, 1938; *Speech and the deaf child*. Manchester, Manchester University Press, 1954.

In the French-speaking countries considerable progress is claimed in the education of the deaf through the use of the methods developed by Professor Guberina of the University of Zagreb. Various sign systems (for example the Paget-Gorman Sign System) and cued speech have been developed with success and have proved useful adjuncts in the learning of communication of all kinds.

33. Descriptions of techniques of parent guidance will be found in: Levy, J. H. A study of parent groups for handicapped children. *Except. child* (University of Queensland), vol. 19, pt. 1, 1952.

34. Dale, D. M. C. (Personal communication.) See also: Dale, op. cit., note 31.

35. Davie, R.; Butler, N.; Goldstein, H. *From birth to seven*. London, Longman, 1972.

36. Ibid.

37. Fraser, G. M.; Blockley, J. *The language disordered child*. Windsor, National Foundation for Educational Research in England and Wales, 1973.

38. Tervoort, Father B. The effectiveness of communication among deaf children as a contribution to mental growth. *In*: Ewing, A. W. G. *The modern educational treatment of deafness*. Manchester, Manchester University Press, 1960.

39. Butler, N.; Peckham, C.; Sheridan, M. Speech defects in children aged 7 years: a national study. *Br. med. j.* (London, British Medical Association), 3 Feb., 1975.

40. That is to say diagnosed as subnormal, recommended for special education or attending special classes.

41. The result in later life of such a double neglect is illustrated by the two following cases of 18-year-olds. The first had twice been to hospital for operations to rectify a cleft palate and a hare-lip at the ages of 6 and 9; he had then attended a speech training clinic part-time for three years, finishing his educational career in a private school at 14. His speech was very blurred, and at 18 he had a pronounced personality difficulty (inferiority feelings, dependence, immaturity), partly centred on a still obvious hare-lip and cleft palate. Though slightly above average in measured general ability, he was able to read no better than a 7-year-old child, and his occupation was the lowest and least skilled form of labouring. The second man, of similar age and of average ability, had so severe a stammer that he twisted his head down to his shoulder with the effort of speech. He was unable to read, even silently, as well as a child of 8. He had attended an ordinary school, but for most of his career there had spent half a day a week attending a speech training clinic. In this case a profound emotional disturbance was at least one of the roots of the speech defect; and he began to make progress both in speech and in reading when efforts were made to readjust his personal difficulties. See: Wall, W. D. Reading backwardness among men in the army. *Br. j. edc. psychol.* (Edinburgh), vol. 15, no. 1, 1945; vol. 16, no. 2, 1946.

42. For example, congenital malformation of the heart occurs in roughly 8 per 1,000 live births but prevalence among children of school age is about 2 per 1,000. (Mande, R.; Masse, N.;

Manciaux, M. op. cit., note 8, chapter 1.) The National Child Development Study's 1958 figure for 7-year-olds is 3·6 per 1,000 (Butler, N.; Davie R.; Goldstein, H. op. cit., note 35).

43. Manciaux, M., et al. Principales maladies chroniques. *In*: Mande, R.; Masse, N.; Manciaux, M. op. cit., note 8, chapter 1.

44. Rutter, M.; Tizard, J.; Whitmore, K. op. cit., note 2, chapter 1. Perhaps the most reliable estimate is that gained by the examination of the 7-year-olds of the National Child Development Study's 1958 longitudinal study (Butler, N.; Davie, R.; Goldstein, H. op. cit., note 35) which was 2·74 per cent, with eczema affecting a further 2·47 per cent.

45. Mitchell, R. G.; Dawson, B. Educational and social characteristics of children with asthma. *Arch. dis. child*. (London, British Medical Association), vol. 48, 1973.

46. Pilling, D. *The child with asthma*. Windsor, National Foundation for Educational Research in England and Wales, 1975. Readers of Marcel Proust will recall his elaborate exploration of his own relationship with his mother.

47. Peckham C. & Parriner. London, National Children's Bureau, 1974. [Mimeo]

48. Yule, W.; Rutter, M. Educational aspects of physical disorder. *In*: Rutter, M.; Tizard, J.; Whitmore, K., eds. op. cit., note 2, chapter 1.

49. Geubelle, F.; Duchesne-Baudouin, A.; Joulet, M. Approche des problèmes medico-sociaux de l'enfant asthmatique. *Acta paediatr. Belg*. (Bruxelles, Association des sociétés scientifiques médicales belges), vol. 21, no. 3, 1967.

50. Mitchel, R. G.; Dawson, B. op. cit., note 44.

51. Mande, R.; Masse, N.; Manciaux, M. op. cit., note 8, chapter 1, p. 419–420. About one-third of cases are of unknown aetiology, about 20 per cent may be hereditary, but most seem to be due to birth injury, some to post-natal injury and early meningitis. The National Child Development Study's 1958 longitudinal survey estimate of prevalence of epilepsy among 7-year-olds is 6·2 per 1,000 (Butler, N.; Davie, R.; Goldstein, H. op. cit., note 35.)

52. Manciaux, M. *In*: Mande, R.; Masse, N.; Manciaux, M. op. cit., note 8, chapter 1, p. 423.

53. There is little evidence for a high rate of emotional disorder among the orthopaedically handicapped, though research does suggest that the physically handicapped may have more difficulty in social relationships and are less mature. Educationally, as we have seen (Chapter 1), such children may be more vulnerable and the little evidence available from the United Kingdom suggests that the attainments of children in special schools are lower than those of the orthopaedically handicapped attending ordinary schools. See: Pilling, D. *The orthopaedically handicapped child*. Slough, National Foundation for Educational Research in England and Wales, 1972.

54. See chapter 1, p. 11.

55. Rhesus incompatibility, for example.

56. Asher, P.; Schonell, F. E. A survey of 400 cases of cerebral palsy in childhood. *Arch. dis. child*. (London, British Medical Association), vol. 25, 1950; Dunsdon, M. I. *The educability of the cerebrally palsied child*. London, National Foundation for Educational Research in England and Wales, 1952. A knowledge of some of the avoidable causes has led to a considerable diminution in incidence, so much so in fact that special schools and units set up by the authorities and by private benevolence have vacant places, which tend to be used for the growing group of children with spina bifida.

   On the other hand, it seems that more children than was thought suffer some kind of damage to the central nervous system which does not result in gross motor handicap but may selectively or generally affect cognitive functioning.

57. A condition in which 'knife clasp' rigidity of muscles results in characteristic stiffness of movement and contractures producing deformity or in some cases an abnormal flaccidity of muscles. According to the number of limbs affected, the condition is called monoplegia, hemiplegia, quadriplegia and (where only the legs are affected) paraplegia. Other terms are used, but these seem to be becoming standard in English and American practice.

58. Characteristically, these show uncontrolled writhing movements, particularly of the limbs, but often of facial and tongue muscles.

59. The assessment of the educability of a cerebrally palsied child calls for great skill and experience from the psychologist, and at present we have no tests which are fully adapted for

use with children who can often indicate no more than a positive or negative response. The author remembers one child of 8 who could make practically no movement except with the toes of his left foot and with his eyes. Nevertheless, in a supine position, he attempted and solved a series of performance tests at a level little below that to be expected of the average child of his own age. Another child, unable to speak or move his limbs, for over three hours ingeniously using his forehead and nose, struggled successfully through certain tests of the Terman-Merrill and Wechsler Bellevue scales and a series of supplementary performance tests, securing an (estimated) I.Q. of 140, which he subsequently justified in his education. See: Brown, C. *My left foot*. London, Secker & Warburg, 1972. See also: note 17 above.

60.   Loring, J., ed. *Assessment of the cerebral palsied child for education*. London, Spastics Society & Heinemann, 1968; Cruickshank, W. M., ed. *The teacher of brain injured children*. New York, Syracuse University Press, 1968.

61.   Consequently, the initiative is often taken by voluntary societies (for example: The Spastics Society, United Kingdom, and the Association des infirmes moteurs cérébraux, France) who succeed in raising considerable sums of money to support schools, special medical treatment, and psychological, medical and educational research.

62.   For example the Carlson House School, Victoria Road, Harborne, Birmingham, which was the earliest in the United Kingdom. Similar initiatives exist in France, in Australia and in the United States, where attention has been concentrated on the problem particularly since Dr Carlson, himself a spastic, became famous. It should be pointed out that there is no direct correlation between the extent of physical or sensory impairment and level of intelligence. Some very retarded children have little physical involvement; some of the most highly intelligent are severe athetoids. A considerable proportion are so little handicapped physically or mentally that, with some degree of medical and psychological supervision, they can profitably attend ordinary or special schools with other children.

63.   Prevalence estimates vary from 4 per 1,000 to 1·5 per 1,000. It has been found that, of such children born between 1959 and 1963 and surviving: 3 per cent had no physical handicap, 15 per cent a moderate handicap, 49 per cent a severe handicap combined with an I.Q. of 80 or above, 21 per cent a severe handicap and I.Q.s in the range 61–79, and 12 per cent an extreme handicap with I.Q.s below 60. Seventy-five per cent of spina bifida children suffer in some degree from hydrocephalus, but since 1958 valve mechanisms have been inserted in the head to drain the excess fluid and thus restrict the damage.

64.   Anderson, Elizabeth Marion, op. cit., note 10, chapter 1, citing Spain, B. Spina bifida survey. *Q. bull.* (London, Greater London Council Research and Intelligence Unit), vol. 12; Miller, E.; Sethi, L. Tactile matching in children with hydrocephalus. *Neuropaediatr.* (Stuttgart), no. 3, 1971; Miller, E.; Sethi, L. The effects of hydrocephalus on perception. *Dev. med. & child neurol.* (London), supplement 25.

65.   Woodburn, M. F. *Social implications of spina bifida*. Windsor, National Foundation for Educational Research in England and Wales, 1975. This research study carried out in south-east Scotland presents a vividly factual and detailed picture of the difficulties, worries and anxieties caused for families and for the children themselves by this complex disability. It also contains a mine of information concerning the ways in which such difficulties can be met.

66.   Woodburn, M. F. op. cit., note 65 (p. 256) and citing Hewitt, S. *The family and the handicapped child*. London, Allen & Unwin, 1970; Pringle, M. L. K.; Fiddes, D. O. *The challenge of thalidomide*. Harlow, Longman, 1970; Schaffer, H. R. The too-cohesive family. *Int. j. soc. psychiat.* (London), vol. 10, no. 4, 1964.

67.   See Hobbs, N. ed. *Issues in the classification of children*. Vol. I and Vol. II. San Francisco, London, Jossey-Bass, 1975, especially part IV (Special perspectives), chapters 20 and 21 ('Effect on parents' and 'Perspectives of the labelled child').

68.   Among *physically handicapped* children—according to the Isle of Wight survey referred to earlier—71 per cent had only one handicap (physical), 14 per cent had two (5·8 per cent educational, 6·6 per cent psychiatric) and 12 per cent three (8 per cent intellectual plus educational; 2·4 per cent intellectual plus psychiatric); and 4 per cent had four. (See: Tizard, J. The epidemiology of handicapping conditions of educational importance. *In*: Pringle, M. L. K.; Varma, V. P. *Advances in educational psychology*, vol. 2. London, U.L.P., 1974.) On the

other hand, studies of actual populations of severely *intellectually retarded* groups suggest that 80 per cent of them have multiple handicaps (Contribution of Mlle. M. T. Georges to the *Séminaire sur les enfants atteints d'insuffisance mentale*. Paris, Centre international de l'enfance, 1972. [Mimeo.]. 20 per cent delicate; 10 per cent with marked sensory defect; 43 per cent with neurological damage; 39 per cent epileptic; 22 per cent psychotic.) Among the Isle of Wight intellectually retarded, 51·7 per cent had two handicaps (46·6 per cent educational as might be expected), 29·3 per cent had three (17 per cent educational plus physical, 5 per cent psychiatric plus physical) and 8·6 per cent had four handicaps. In all, 84·5 per cent have an educational handicap, 22·4 a psychiatric one, and 34·4 per cent a physical one.

69.   High tone deafness, undetectable by the somewhat gross methods of diagnosing hearing loss in general use, may hinder or prevent the development of intelligible speech and make some of the discriminations involved in reading difficult to make. Children with this and other kinds of auditory difficulty are being more readily detected now by the use of pure tone audiometers, but cases are all too frequently still found of intelligent children labouring along among the dull or even markedly subnormal, consigned there on a superficial diagnosis (based perhaps on a whisper test or a watch tick in a noisy room) which failed to detect high frequency loss. The testing of the special senses by the various psycho-physical methods now available is a skilled process requiring, with children at all events, a sound training in child psychology as well as a knowledge of physiology and of the instruments used.

70.   A certain amount of significant research suggests that marked clumsiness and some disturbances of the visual field—poor and disorderly development of visual perception—of attention, of the finger and body schema, of apperception of sound sequences, of patterns, of rapid figure-ground discrimination during tachistoscopic presentation, of the ability to sort according either to logical or formal elements, etc., which are found either generally or selectively among groups with identifiable cortical damage, can also be shown to exist in children without any demonstrable neurological damage but who do present specific learning difficulties in arithmetic and reading. See: Bender, L. *Visual motor gestalt test*. New York. American Orthopsychiatric Association, 1938 (Research monograph, no. 3); Doll, E. A.; Phelps, W. M.; Melcher, R. *Mental deficiency due to birth injuries*. New York, Macmillan, 1932; Lord, E.; Wood, L. Diagnostic values in a visuo-motor test, *Am. j. orthopsychiatr*. (New York, American Orthopsychiatric Association), 1942; Goldstein, K.; Scheerer, M. *Abstract and concrete behaviour*. New York, Johnson Reprint Corp., 1941. (Psych. monographs, vol. 53, no. 2). Strauss, A. A.; Lechtinen, L. E. *Psychopathology and education of the brain-injured child*. New York, Grune & Stratton, 1950–57; Francis-Williams, J. M. W. *Children with specific learning difficulties: the effect of neuro-developmental learning disorders on children of normal intelligence*. Oxford, Pergamon, 1970; Cruickshank, W. M. *The brain-injured child in home, school and community*. London, Pitman, 1971; Dinnage, R. *The handicapped child: research review*. Vol. 1. Harlow, Longman, in association with the National Bureau for Co-operation in Child Care, 1970.

71.   The educational and personal guidance of any handicapped child and of his family—particularly in the very large proportion of cases where the diagnosis is by no means clear—is not something which can be done by snap medical, psychological or any other kind of brief examination. There is a need for diagnostic teaching and observation over a period of time and this is best done for the very young child through diagnostic units integrated with good nursery and infant schools. See Chapter II of this book.

72.   Of the thirty-eight countries replying to a Unesco 'Questionnaire on special education' (*A study of the recent situation of special education*. Paris, 1971, Unesco FD/MD/16. [Mimeo]), a number of the more advanced (notably France and the United States) drew attention to the ways in which extensive systems of special education tend to regard categorization of children.

Chapter three

Psychological growth: home and family

DEFECT, DISABILITY AND HANDICAP

Many individuals have defects of their physical organism, congenital or acquired in the course of growth—a deformation of the outer ear for example, colour-anomalous vision, a delicate constitution like Sir Walter Scott, a club foot like Byron or a limp like Talleyrand—which do not necessarily constitute a disability, still less a major handicap. There are others whose defects in locomotion, in the sensory organs, in the central nervous system, or in major organs of the body like the heart or lungs, do under almost any circumstances constitute disabilities and lead to physical malfunctioning which may or may not persist over a long time, and may or may not distort normal growth, development, learning and adjustment to life. Only if a defect or, more usually, a disability permanently retards or distorts general development can we accurately speak of it as a handicap.

This may seem to be something of a semantic quibble, but it is more than this. Any defect, however slight, can in fact grow into a handicap—particularly if its presence becomes a source of exaggerated concern to the individual and those around him, and little is done positively to mitigate its effects. Some at least of the personality characteristics of Scott, Byron or Talleyrand can be traced to the psychological meanings their disabilities acquired for them, though they did not constitute serious handicaps. The very treatment of a defect or disability may, by preventing a child from activity or experience essential to his growth, induce an accumulating handicap. There are some defects and disabilities, notably impairments of the central nervous system, which almost inevitably seem to be handicapping in the sense that they disorganize or inhibit learning even when special measures are taken. Others, like motor handicap, blindness and deafness, certainly interpose serious obstacles to normal cognitive, social and emotional growth especially in infancy and childhood. But, at least theoretically, they do not prevent a reasonably normal course of development if steps are taken soon enough to mitigate their effects. In many other conditions, although the disability or constellation of disabilities is clearly gravely handicapping to anything like normal development, a great deal can be done to prevent the more serious psychological and educational consequences. Any condition, however mild or serious, becomes more or less severely handicapping according to how far those around the child—family, school, medical and social workers—are able to understand the meaning of the disability to the child and take steps to see that the essential emotional, social and conceptual experiences underlying successful learning are provided, in spite of the disability.

There are, however, distinctions to be made. Children with physical defects of any kind, of greater or lesser severity, present educational and mental health problems of a different order from those of the genuinely intellectually retarded and dull. It is true, of course, that some, even many, physically handicapped children are, because of central nervous system damage, mentally subnormal as well—in certain types of case, notably cerebral palsy, this is frequently so. Conversely, as we have seen, minor or major physical handicaps, organic inferiorities, chronic disorders and the like, are frequently found to accompany profound, severe, moderate and to a lesser extent mild, intellectual retardation—that is, they are part of a mental and physical syndrome of what is sometimes called general organic inferiority.

But it is nevertheless also true to say that groups of motor-impaired children, or children with peripheral visual or auditory defects, and most of those with chronic diseases like asthma or diabetes, haemophiliacs and those with defective or anomalous major organs which render them more vulnerable than ordinary children, seem likely, *under reasonably favourable circumstances*, to have a distribution of general ability to learn which is much the same as that found in the population as a whole. In all too many cases, however, one of the cumulative effects of the educational neglect of the disability, particularly in the crucial first three years, is a severe dulling of intelligence itself and the power to learn. Even where this is not markedly so, what we frequently do find—as the inquiries reported in Chapter One show—is that their attainments in school are noticeably lower than might be expected from their general ability. The proportions of maladjustment and behaviour difficulty also seem to be higher than is general among unhandicapped groups.

Some, but not all, of this is because the physical condition of handicapped children often involves a period of hospitalization and convalescence, continuing attendance at clinics for treatment, restrictions or prohibitions on mobility, and diets or drug treatments which interrupt or make difficult the smooth flow of early development and disturb education in an ordinary school or class, or even a special school.

DISABILITY AS A CAUSE OF DEPRIVATION

Such obvious practical difficulties imposed by general delicateness of constitution, chronic disorder, disease or weakness, or by a physical disability, must not, however, lead us to neglect the more subtle and ultimately more important repercussions of a defect upon the child's whole psychological development. For example, the importance of walking for emotional and intellectual development in the second year has only to be recalled to see that a crippled child dependent upon others for mobility may lack a vital stimulus to growth simply because he cannot move freely in the exploration of his environment. Later, as he becomes aware of his difference from others, and as progressively he lacks the confirmation of security that the ordinary child gains from physical achievement and praise, his personality development may begin to deviate. Obscurely, he may come to feel that his disability is a punishment and develop a feeling of guilt; or he may become by turns aggressive against his environment or fearful of it in a vague, anxious way. Because of the over-protective attitudes of their parents, of other adults and even of their teachers and fellow pupils, many physically handicapped or delicate children find refuge in their disability and use it as an excuse to avoid tasks which they could well perform. Thus, among the handicapped, one finds not a few who exploit their condition to reduce a parent or relative to a state of slavery and who become parasitic on a community to which, with different handling, they could have made a contribution.

THE IMPORTANCE OF THE EARLY YEARS

Normal children by the age of 5 or 6 have already accomplished many of the main feats of growth and learning. They have gained a very considerable command of their bodies, can run and jump, balance and climb; their hands, although still by no means finely co-ordinated, nonetheless work well with their eyes and enable them to accomplish considerable tasks like building towers with bricks or making meaningful drawings. The 5- or 6-year-old has mastered a very complex grammatical and syntactical linguistic structure, can communicate his wishes, give and receive simple orders and already possesses a considerable vocabulary with which to label, recall and manipulate concepts of many concrete kinds. He or she will have gained a measure of independence in such things as toileting, dressing, eating, and will usually be able to control impulses and tolerate the mother's absence for quite long periods and in unfamiliar surroundings. Five- or six-year-olds delight in social play with others, in shared fantasy and conversation, in co-operative games with increasingly complex rules. They will have ideas about themselves as being good, bad, successful, unsuccessful, acceptable and loved—a whole self-image and self-esteem in which their security and readiness to venture forth to tackle new challenges is rooted. They are, for the most part, on the threshold of an effective style of concrete operational thinking which will enable them to learn how to predict and manipulate that part of the real world which they can see and touch, and which mainly (but not solely) they can reason logically about through language and share with parents, teachers and other children. No other period of life—except possibly the early years of puberty—is so crammed with new physical, social, emotional and intellectual acquisitions; and no other period is so totally crucial as a foundation for all that follows.

Learning of all these many and complex kinds depends upon three things. The steady maturation of the physical organism which, for example, readies the baby for reaching out and handling, crawling, then walking erect, and later for many feats of agility and co-ordination. A part of this growth is ascribable to the increasing usefulness and maturation in the senses of hearing, vision and, to a lesser extent, touch and kinaesthesis. These senses, particularly sight and hearing, enable the child to build up percepts and then concepts of objects and relationships of people and places; thus his intelligence and knowledge of the world is constructed. As his central nervous system and his physical apparatus mature they enable him to do more things; the doing of more and different things structures and shapes his maturation.

But physical and physiological maturation alone do not ensure satisfactory development. Like any other animal, the young human grows and learns from his material environment. The outside world of plants and flowers, huts or houses, cars or bullock carts, animals and objects of all kinds, and so on, provokes his interest, motivates his growth and learning, and provides the stream of percepts from which he elaborates the conceptual structure of his mind. If the material environment is markedly impoverished for any reason, or if the child's interaction with it is grossly interfered with—because he cannot explore by movement or by touch, because he cannot see—then the perceptual–conceptual 'bricks' with which he should build the whole framework of cognition are just not there or are made extremely difficult to come by.

The third crucial element in early growth is the human one—usually the parents and immediate family of brothers, sisters and relatives. For a normally equipped and developing child, his family is a filter, a buffer and a bridge. From this group, and particularly from the mother, the child acquires his early language, his ideas about himself and others, his scale of values and meanings and the crucial foundations of his education in the wide sense. And we know that the influence of this family background is predominant in all kinds of learning, at least to the end of adolescence.

As we have seen,[1] this process of socialization of the young child, even if he is physically intact, is unlikely to be fully satisfactory in terms of optimal growth if it is left to the light of nature. Many otherwise normal children are deprived of their full potential development by the inefficiency and inadequacy of their parents, by the fact that their environment is disorganized or lacking in essential experiences. A disability or a defect, particularly if it directly affects locomotion or one of the special senses, interposes in the task of good parenting a major obstacle which requires imagination, knowledge and ingenuity well beyond what most adults have or can develop unaided. If the child's defect is not confined to the peripheral sense organs or mechanisms of locomotion, but directly interferes with those parts of the cerebral cortex concerned with cognition and learning, and with the inhibition and elaboration of impulse, it may be difficult indeed for the parents to maintain an accepting, loving and calm relationship with their child, to give the kind of assurance and support which, more even than a healthily developing child, the handicapped require as the very foundation of their chances of satisfactory development.

A POSITIVE APPROACH

Crucial, therefore, in the development of a handicapped child is an effort to normalize and enrich an environment made abnormal and depriving by the child's defect. It is in this sense then that we can speak of a special pedagogy of the early years of growth. The essential emphasis is on building upon and exploiting what the child can do in such a way as to provide him with the experience and stimulus to growth of which his condition would otherwise deprive him. Thus, though the child who cannot walk, run or jump is in danger of being deprived both of the widening range of experience and of the praise which physical acquirements bring more or less spontaneously to the young, his life can be organized by an intelligent mother to give him equivalent experience and similar stimulus. To do this, she, or some professionally trained person in contact with her, needs both a wide and accurate knowledge of how normal children develop psychologically and an imaginative understanding of the circumstances of the individual child concerned. This is even more important ultimately than, for example, a crutch or physiotherapy.

What seems to be decisive is a basic change of attitude among professionals so that the psychological needs of the child and his family are given priority over medical and administrative convenience, and that every essential intervention or continuing course of treatment is most carefully evaluated in a wide, developmental context and conducted with the least possible disturbance to that sequence of experiences essential to the normal growth of any child—and even more important for those already at a disadvantage.

Many handicapped children, for example, undergo physical pain at an early age, are made to lie for long periods immobile staring at the ceiling or are taken off to hospital and separated from their mothers. Certainly, the efficient administration of medical treatment is made easier if the child can be handled as if he were a physical organism without psychological reactions. But, in the long run, it may be better to delay an operation in hospital until the child can understand and tolerate absence from his mother, to allow mother to enter hospital with her child or even for the medical team to accept the inconvenience of carrying out the operation and subsequent supervision at the child's home.

Similarly, a child should always be sensitively prepared for the experience of pain, and be reassured that it means neither punishment nor aggression. Where, as sometimes happens, his movement has to be restricted almost completely for a period, steps should be taken to reduce to a minimum the emptiness of the hours, not merely to avoid boredom, but to ensure that intellectual and emotional growth is not impeded at a critical moment. When the time of restriction is past, such a child should, as far as possible, be given enriched opportunities to make up lost development. The limitations imposed by any continuing physical treatment, particularly if it is painful, should be carefully examined first to see if it is strictly essential and then in terms of its psychological effect upon the child, and upon the attitudes and possibilities of his family. It will often be found that the rigour can be mitigated when understanding and ingenuity are used. There are, too, many ways in which handicapped children and their parents can be helped to concentrate upon what can be achieved rather than upon the limitations and burdens imposed by disability. Sometimes an operation which may be medically desirable should even be abandoned or postponed and the physical limitation accepted rather than taking the risk of a gross disturbance of a vital stage of growth, in such a way as to prejudice later development irreparably.

GUIDANCE AND EDUCATION

This kind of psychological guidance of a physically handicapped child and of his family is a delicate and skilled business. Medical skill has, of course, a major contribution to make, usually in the initial stages of diagnosis and restorative treatment, but it is by no means the sole or even in many cases the dominant one. The future of the child depends upon the highest achievement possible for him of personal, social, educational and vocational adjustment. If he is fully to hold his own with others, this adjustment must be at a level at least as high as, if not higher than, that of his unhandicapped compeers. To do this, he and his parents need well-informed and sympathetic help throughout his growth, and all treatment and education should be planned in a holistic, co-ordinated way. This can only be done by those who, aware of the limits imposed by the disability, are equipped by their training to consider the child as a whole person with needs of the same order as those of normal children. The family counsellor, the educational expert, the paediatrician and the psychologist have a role in this, not only at the initial examination, but in the continuing supervision of such children. Indeed, as the critical phases of strictly physical treatment pass, it is the psychologist and the educator who should accept the principal responsibility.[2]

It is clear that, just as a physical difficulty should not be considered in isolation from the general psychological and developmental needs of a child, so a disabled child cannot be satisfactorily helped if he is considered as an individual case divorced from the context of his family. The prime educators of the child are his or her parents, and in the first three or so years of life they are almost the sole educators. On their skill and insight depends very much of any child's future capacity to cope with life and make the most of what capacities and qualities he possesses. Disability and the anxiety it provokes, the interference with ordinary routines and the burden imposed usually on the mother, by medical treatment and by the continuing care many such children need, are very disruptive of family life. Even when material circumstances in the home are good, and the family a united and supportive one, there is inevitably a great deal of strain—and it is a strain which, unlike the ordinary crises of childhood illness, looks to have no end. There is, too, in spite of considerable welfare provision, an additional financial burden imposed by handicap. Where the family is poor, the mother not very well educated and weighed down with the cares of clothing and feeding other children, the financial burden may force her even more to neglect the psychological needs of her handicapped child.

For most families, a handicapped child in their midst is a unique experience; no one can learn what to do for the best by the simple light of love and nature. Nor, except by rare happy accident, can the subtle and understanding developmental help required by—for example—a blind or motor-handicapped child be given by parents who, at most, have had five minutes of general conversation with a busy paediatrician or general practitioner, and perhaps an hour with a social worker. What is needed is the development of realistic, immediate and long-term goals for the child in collaboration with the parents, the construction of a plan of upbringing which compensates as far as possible for the deprivations imposed by the handicap, and a sustained effort of support and consultation over the whole developmental period—a support which provides the family with an expert consultant partner, particularly valuable at crisis periods and at points where important decisions have to be made.

Of recent years, in Europe and North America, associations concerned with specific handicaps have grown up. Many of them concern themselves with arousing public interest in the area of handicap concerned, bringing pressure to bear on the authorities to make more adequate provision, and with the promotion of research and the dissemination of information. Even more valuable to individual families, however, is the bringing of parents with similar or complementary problems into contact with each other for mutual support and assistance. Many fathers and mothers who have had experience of handicap in their own families, for example, make excellent and supportive counsellors to others. Groups of parents band together to provide facilities which no family could supply on its own. Special apparatus, toys and so on can be exchanged. What perhaps is even more important is that such groups help to combat the sense of isolation in the face of an overwhelming problem—the depression which at one time or another threatens to crush the parents of a handicapped child.

PUBERTY AND ADOLESCENCE[3]

At no point in life is understanding, guidance and counselling more necessary than in adolescence. Even the non-handicapped may have a period of difficulty in coming to terms with their physical, sexual, social and vocational roles, and in developing a satisfactory over-all interpretation of what life is all about and their part in it. A physical handicap of any kind directly affects all aspects of the self, and a mental handicap, even a comparatively mild one, makes it more difficult for a young person to analyse, understand and accept the kinds of fantasies and feelings, the demands and constraints imposed by pubertal change interacting with the social pressures which surround him. The physical and psychological changes of puberty, particularly the hormonal ones, and the rapid growth in height, weight and in the sexual characteristics and apparatus, may be delayed or aberrant and—particularly where central nervous system damage is present, or where there is disease or dysfunction of major organs or of the endocrine system—cause alarming changes in behaviour, lead to a resurgence in acute form or change in old symptoms. Moreover, the greater vulnerability of the handicapped as a group to emotional disturbance makes many of them more than normally unstable in adolescence.

Psychologically speaking, what happens to any individual, particularly whether the outcome is generally favourable or unfavourable in adolescence and in adulthood, will very much depend upon previous experiences at home, in school and in society generally and upon how far, during his development, a child has built up an objectively favourable picture of himself and his possibilities. The mental health of handicapped people depends in large measure on this ability to accept others and be accepted by them. Where school and home have placed an accent upon the acceptability of differences between individuals without labelling them inferiorities or superiorities, and without either rejecting the handicapped or sentimentalizing over them, there is a good chance that most will be equipped to draw the essential distinction between the value of human being *per se* and the variety of capacities which makes human groups unequal in their responsibilities and needs. The attainment of such a goal requires from teachers, parents and others round the children and adolescents not only a high degree of pedagogic skill but a knowledge of human development, and an ability sensitively to diagnose capacity in many directions for which few are at present trained. Beyond everything else, it requires the capacity to create a climate in which each child is certain that he is valued for what he is, and that his achievements, however small, are acceptable to those on whom he depends, and win him the esteem of the group.

THE PHYSICAL SELF

One of the critical emotional problems of those who are physically handicapped, particularly if they are deformed or disfigured, is that of accepting themselves physically as they are. Many such children have disordered body schemas; most, consciously or unconsciously, at some time experience guilt at their handicap, resentment at the restriction it imposes, and may project some of their aggressions painfully upon parents or others close to them—particularly under the normal impulses of adolescence towards personal autonomy. On the other hand, dependence may increase and be coupled with anxiety and fear at one's own helplessness, or the child may retreat into fantasies in which he is dramatically made whole. Certainly, pubertal changes and the reaction of others to them increase bodily awareness and self-consciousness. For parent and child alike, the acceptance of handicap is made more difficult if they have been fed upon false hopes of normality or near normality. The problem can also be increased if the children are told they 'will grow out of it', and if throughout childhood as well as in adolescence they are not given, sympathetically, an adequate, detailed and objective appraisal of what is and is not possible and of how far a particular handicap does or does not permit the hope of a particular vocation.

SEXUAL ADJUSTMENT

Closely linked with notions of the physical self, but even more complex in its ramifications, is the problem of sexuality, love, marriage and founding a family. In some cases, of course—for example spina bifida—sexuality may be profoundly interfered with, or a major handicap render anything approaching normal intercourse mechanically impossible; but in most cases there is no inherent reason to think a reasonably normal sex life to be impossible, though there may be genetic reasons[4] against child-bearing; or, as in the case of girls with severe heart conditions for example, great difficulty or danger involved.

But the achievement of a satisfactory and satisfying sexual adjustment is very much more than this. It lies at the very centre of a whole web of social relationships ranging from love and friendship to the series of adjustments underlying a broad social role. Its roots lie in attitudes to the self and others built up over the whole of life. Quite apart from those in whom damage to their central nervous system is itself responsible for personality, behavioural or emotional difficulties, all handicapped children from their earliest years are, by the circumstances of their handicap, more vulnerable to insecurities, anxieties and feelings of worthlessness; in one degree or another all are likely to have difficulties, within themselves or because of the reactions of those around them (particularly from the general public) in forming healthy personal relationships.[5] Parents of handicapped children would be less than human if they did not fundamentally resent the handicap, wish their child normal, feel anxious and insecure, and at times bewildered, ashamed and guilty. Sometimes these feelings turn into an over-possessive, over-protective attitude which may itself become as damaging as the handicap and cut the child, and later the adolescent or adult he becomes, off from any hope of social intercourse outside his own restricted circle.

Thus the attainment of a satisfactory sexual and social self depends upon how far parents can be helped, right from the outset, to understand and meet the emotional needs of their child. How far, for example, can they at critical times, like periods of hospitalization or pain in early childhood, assuage the child's often unexpressed and even unconscious fear that this is a punishment for his own wickedness; or how can they help the child who is frustrated by his own clumsiness, or who feels himself the object of ridicule by other children? Too little is done to help parents of handicapped children to face and come to terms with their own unconscious attitudes and fears, and to develop a deep insight into the needs of their children. At puberty and adolescence, counselling of the child and his parents of a supportive and interpretive sort, concerned with social relations and with sex, is just as important, if not more so, as guidance of conventional kinds.

VOCATIONAL ADJUSTMENT

Economic independence is important to self-respect and may be essential to marriage. To the handicapped, the best degree of autonomy and responsibility possible for them is one of the foundations of a feeling of worth, and a source of reassurance against the day when the parents are no longer there. Many handicapped persons will, of course, never be fully self-supporting and able to compete with success on the open market; but there are proportionately few who cannot contribute something of value. Again, the foundations for this are laid early by encouraging independence in dressing and feeding, in movement about the house and neighbourhood without supervision, in accepting a graded and increasing responsibility for possessions, for animals and for other people, at school and eventually at work. It is of the utmost importance to recognize that the very existence of a handicap implies what has been called the creation of 'plus value' by education so far as this is possible: to be equal to the non-handicapped, the handicapped person must, paradoxically, in some ways be better. This implies careful planning of education and subsequently of vocational training so that any strengths are maximized and that vocational goals are realistically set and accepted emotionally by the adolescent and his family, whether this is ultimately open employment, some kind of sheltered occupation, work at home or an occupation which is barely remunerable. Specialized vocational guidance at school-leaving is obviously essential and is increasingly being provided by youth employment services. But the guidance of a handicapped person must begin long before the end of the compulsory educational period. It should be part of an ongoing process of self-appraisal and self-development in which family and school are progressively involved from childhood.

Adjustments in all these areas—physical, sexual, social and vocational—will be determined as much, if not more, by how children or adolescents feel about themselves and their handicaps as they will by the nature, or even by the degree, of handicaps involved.[6] Ultimately, then, we are concerned to help the handicapped to develop, as satisfactorily as possible, a moral, ethical or philosophic self which integrates in a positive way the other roles and aspects of the self in adolescence. And here the same considerations apply as to normally healthy children and adolescents, but with perhaps even more urgency. An education which, as well as providing essential instrumental and vocational skills, constructs the essential modes of thought and feeling which enable an understanding of the work of people and things gives a measure of intellectual and personal autonomy, and feeds the adolescent need to construct ideals and test them against realities, is, if anything, more necessary to the handicapped than to others. More necessary, too, is the chance to talk out with a sympathetic adult and at the adolescent's own level the problems, fears and uncertainties which come to any adolescent and which the handicapped experience in an acute form with many additional complexities.

Education, vocational training and placement, social integration and personal adjustment are made much more difficult by even a slight handicap. Moreover, any aspect of development may be actually slower with many handicaps and even at the age of 15 or 16 the child may be conspicuously immature for his age in some or all respects. There may also be marked discrepancies between physical and intellectual development, or between either of these and emotional growth. Some prolongation of broadly educational influence and certainly of personal guidance beyond the legal end of compulsory schooling is therefore likely to be essential to many handicapped adolescents. What is needed is an expert 'friend' to help them cope with the transition from the shelter of school into a wider and more impersonal world.

We have concentrated so far on two critical periods of growth—early childhood and adolescence. In different ways these are more formative than the periods in between, because important cognitive and emotional changes are then taking place and with considerable rapidity. For example, the onset of puberty in normal children is marked by some very rapid changes in the physiological and physical mechanism, increases in height and weight, changes in the hormonal balance and enhancement of such fundamental drives as sex or aggressiveness. There may be quite striking cognitive changes too; the development of abstract conceptual thinking which has an important bearing not only on what the young adolescent will be interested in, but upon the development of attitudes, moral and personal judgements and so on.

Very early childhood—the first three or so years—is equally a period of very rapid and dramatic development, physically and cognitively. As has been indicated earlier, it tends to be heavily determinant both of the general level of intellectual ability and of what might be called general coping styles. Children are, of course, vulnerable to disturbance at any stage of growth. Equally, it cannot be said that nothing can be done to improve matters, if necessary, after early childhood. What does seem to be true is that, the earlier the intervention, the better the chances of success and the less massive our efforts have to be. But the work done in attempting to compensate for the effects of early deprivation has also shown that efforts confined to any particular period of growth—the pre-school period or, indeed, to adolescence—though they may produce a considerable immediate increase in function or amelioration of personality, tend to be largely negated unless they are followed up by support over a long period.

In most cases it is not possible, and probably not desirable, that this continuous support should be so massive as to take the child out of the responsibility of its family. Yet we know that, in most circumstances, the influence of the family on the over-all development of its children is something like three times as powerful as that of any other institution; and that, in a somewhat different way in later years, this is broadly true from birth to well into the second decade. Hence, while we may improve the schools and provide the handicapped with more intensive and continuing support over the growth years, we are not likely to achieve full success unless the family itself, and particularly the parents, become highly skilled educators of their own children.

It is for this reason that the idea of a continuous consultative relationship between a well-qualified worker and the family has been advocated. But, manifestly, such a relationship requires much more than conventional social work skills and a much more profound practical knowledge, both of normal child development and of the difficulties of all kinds imposed by handicap, than is usually possessed, even by those who deal with the social aspects of families with a handicapped child. And one would suggest that such a person's role is one which straddles the educational and social fields, as well as acting as a liaison with the appropriate medical services and, when necessary, with those concerned with economic aid and such matters as housing. Since the school system is the major official institution directly concerned with all children and with their families, and since the main thrust of the task we are talking about is educational in the broadest possible sense, one would expect such workers to be part of the educational services, moving in and out of schools and pre-school organizations quite freely, and bringing the health and social services into contact with the schools.

The education of the parents of a handicapped child would not be a formal process— a matter of a few sessions in some sort of clinic, supported perhaps by pamphlets and occasional good advice. It would be carried out by interaction between the trained and knowledgeable worker and the parents over the day-to-day management of the child, and centred upon a co-operative relationship to determine goals and means of ensuring a favourable development. Supplementary help of many kinds would, of course, also be necessary. For example, it has been found valuable to arrange for parents, or better still whole families, and their handicapped child to stay for a short time in specialized clinics or schools. These can give an overtaxed mother something of a respite, give a feeling that there are others with similar or even more serious problems, and provide the possibility of training parents or elder children in some of the more difficult ways of helping the handicapped. Mutual aid between parents can also be organized with the help of a third party in a great variety of ways, and particularly so that some parents can get away for a short holiday whilst others take over their child, or indeed so that family holidays, often difficult simply for physical reasons, can in fact be arranged. Even such mundane but very important matters as transporting a handicapped child to and from school or clinic can be greatly simplified if groups of parents work together.

It is often not appreciated, even by those whose professional work brings them into close contact with the families of the handicapped, how greatly the whole climate and mentality of parents and other children are affected by the presence in their midst of someone who may be at least partially dependent well beyond the normal span of childhood and adolescence. Unless one has lived with the difficult and unpleasant domestic tasks imposed, for example, by a child or adolescent who is incontinent, or who has to be helped everywhere, or who is intellectually subnormal and possibly unstable, and therefore cannot be left unattended sometimes even for brief periods, it is difficult to realize how great is the emotional stress, how unrelenting the demand upon time and attention. To this is often added the experience of the revulsion or pity that strangers show, or the ambivalent sentimentality-rejection of friends and relatives. Other children in the family would be scarcely human if they did not resent both the claims on their parents' attention and the profound limitations on their own lives caused by a handicapped member. Similarly, the inevitable tiredness of the parents, their fears and anxieties in the present and for the future, put a great strain on any marriage.

In spite of a much wider appreciation of how disabilities come about and of their consequences, there is nonetheless a great deal of what can only be called 'folklore' and myths. The notion that handicap is a punishment from God is by no means dead and, very often in spite of categoric assurances to the contrary, the belief continues to exist that the disability or defect is due to bad genetic influences in the family of the other partner. Sometimes, too, there is a feeling of guilt on the part of the mother about a slight fall while pregnant, perhaps an attempted abortion, or an indulgence in drink or the use of a drug, or even for the existence of tension with her husband. Sometimes such feelings have a basis in fact, sometimes not. In others the cause is projected on to the doctor who attended (or failed to attend) the birth, or on to the hospital which acted too late or too soon to induce labour. If one listens to the fantasies of parents, it is surprising to note the numbers of doctors who attend confinements having come from some sort of wild party! Most usually, such causes or explanations have little to do with the actual condition of the child; but the guilt or aggressive feelings persist and must be reckoned with as at least an unconscious sub-stratum to parental feelings and attitudes.

This is a whole difficult and subtle area of feeling and attitude, of guilt and anxiety, and sometimes of frustration at the inexorable injustice and cruelty of fate. The family counsellor should be aware of it and equipped at least to reduce its impact upon the parents and, through them, on their child. Some parents can and do deal with it alone, at least at one level, by a religious interpretation and resignation. Others find a kind of fulfilment in a total devotion to the needs of their child, and undertake a kind of dedicated slavery which concentrates their own lives and often those of the whole family on the one object—a basically unhealthy situation for all concerned. Yet others pass from expert to expert, following this hopeful trend or that, this rumour of a miracle drug or that new form of treatment, hoping against hope to get something to hang on to. Yet others hawk their child from hospital to hospital, clinic to clinic, in the attempt to get a diagnosis or a label which will clearly rid them of their feeling of guilt or stigma. They may then devote their energies to the attempt to get some form of special provision which makes their child 'interesting' and more socially acceptable.

All of these forms of reaction are understandable, and the line between an acceptable, even noble, self-sacrifice without sentimentality and the kind of self-pitying over-compensation which does little good to the child is a very fine one. It is hard to take fully into account the fact that a family with a handi-capped child consists of a number of people, all of them with needs and rights, and that any solution to the difficulties imposed which does not bring about a reasonable and fair compromise all round is likely to be unhealthy in one way or another.

One of the most important tasks of those who work with such families is in fact to get the parents and, so far as they are able, the children to reach such a genuine compromise and to view their own and the handicapped child's situa-tion without sentimentality and as objectively as possible. It has to be realized too that, as the handicapped child and his parents grow older, the nature of any compromise should change and the adjustments made at an earlier stage will have to be thought out again and again with the passage of time. Clearly this is not something which can be done by prescription from the outside: and it may be difficult for a family to do it simply by discussion among its members. The outsider who is both sympathetic and informed, skilled in allowing feelings to be expressed, even the difficult and rebellious feelings of which one is ashamed, and who can introduce the experience of others, can help a family group to reach solutions which are practical and acceptable compromises of all the legitimate interests concerned. Such a person can provide that atmosphere of security and confidence which will allow each member of the family to face the anxieties, fears, guilt feelings and the like which, unless they are faced and dealt with, may deeply prejudice any sensible solution and prejudice the mental health of each individual.

One of the most difficult problems, general to the whole field of handicap, but particularly applicable to infantile autism, some kinds of cerebral palsy, and moderate and mild intellectual retardation, is that of how and to what extent hope of improvement should be given to parents, and how far they should be encouraged to become involved in complex and time-consuming activities which may or may not prove to be beneficial to their child. It is, alas, still true that parents are sometimes assured with authority that 'he will grow out of it', or alternatively that there is nothing that can be done. 'Experts', too, will speak with different voices, sometimes giving the answer which they think will, at least temporarily, assuage parental anxiety. There is, as Eisenberg points out,[7] no behaviour that cannot be changed: there is no person who cannot improve given a modest target. But it is crucial to stress, not a pessimistic, but a realistic and cautious view of what can be done, even if it is little; and to set out very fully indeed what that little really may imply in terms of time, effort, sacrifice and dedication. What should certainly not be done is to involve parents, relatives and friends in elaborate and exhausting treatments or systems of handling unless there is very good hope of a pay-off. In fact, where the hope of improvement is slight or where the improvement itself is likely in any case to be small by ordinary standards, the parents may become deeply afflicted with guilt at their lack of success.

Another problem of a different kind arises from the fact that many handicapped children—particularly those who are mildly subnormal and many of those with minor sensory defects and motor handicaps—come from families low on the socio-economic scale and where the mother is herself depressed,[8] lethargic or suffering from a feeling of hopelessness to which the birth of a handicapped child merely adds. Such families, as has been repeatedly shown,[9] make less use of the available health and social services than do others, and tend to provide educational environments which are depriving even for normally endowed children. These families with multiple problems are also the most difficult to bring into anything like active co-operation with home-based schemes.[10]

American and British experience in so-called compensatory education programmes and other efforts to raise the general level of mothering in depressed groups has stressed the value of carefully devised educational home-visiting services.[11]

'AT RISK' REGISTERS, EARLY CASE-FINDING AND PREVENTION

Most deficits or disabilities are present at birth or arise in the early years of life, and much handicap is the result of an interaction of a disability with the early family environment. Parents may be ignorant of the special needs the defect creates or the deprivation it imposes—and unaware, for example, of the way in which enlightened concentration on speech training may help to prevent an auditory deficit leading to a major learning disability, or of the need to enlarge the experience of a child with a motor disability. Many apparently mild defects do not make themselves clearly apparent until damage has been done which could have been prevented by wise guidance of the parents.

Recent longitudinal studies[12] have shown that it is possible to define very early in life groups of children who seem to be 'at risk' and who may become educational problems unless such early preventive measures are taken. The suggestion has been made that some kind of 'at risk' register[13] should be compiled from antenatal and perinatal data. This, it is held, should be supplemented by diagnostic work carried out through the maternal and child welfare services in the pre-school period, and during the first years in the nursery and infant schools. Certainly, anything which enables us to identify children with physical, mental or social defects or difficulties early enough for constructive and preventive help to be given seems highly desirable, before a disability is made into a handicap by neglect.

However, too rigidly systematic registers of this kind are open to objection. A fully adequate, routine, paediatric and psychological screening of all children in their early years would be a daunting task in terms of money and skilled staff; nor would it necessarily be fully efficient. Some children, for example, although their physical and social circumstances would indicate a risk, will not in fact prove to need help; some will be wrongly diagnosed; for others the implied process of labelling may produce the very consequences it seeks to avoid. Probably the best and most practicable way forward is to bring about an increased sensitivity, alertness and knowledge in all those who have to do with young children professionally (medical, social and particularly educational staff who are apt to exclude the pre-school from their preoccupations). A special operational responsibility rests on two groups: the health and social workers who care for mother and child in the earliest years of life; and those educators and others in day-care centres, pre-school play groups, nursery and infant schools who watch over the young child's earliest learning outside his family. If the professionals in direct contact with the young child and his parents can learn to distinguish those children whose development is showing abnormal deviation, can use their skills and insight to help the parents develop an effective educational style, and have the possibility to call upon expert psychological and paediatric help, it seems likely that the outlook for many handicapping conditions—even quite severe ones—will be markedly more optimistic than it is at present. What is more, since many of the necessary services and staff already exist, in developed countries at least, the principal problem in achieving this is not so much one of resources but of the proper training of staff and of breaking the inhibiting professional barriers between education, social work and health.[14]

SERVICES

The kind of family counsellor we have recommended is likely to be most successful if he or she can make contact with the family early and if he or she represents, as it were, the human face of a fully co-ordinated service ready to provide the many specialized forms of help—psychological, educational, social, economic—which are from time to time necessary. Unhappily, such services as exist tend to be fragmented and bureaucratized, and few, even among the highly developed countries, have a full range of services for the handicapped; and in many there is a fundamental confusion of attitudes towards handicapped people, much as there is towards minority groups in general. In many ways, the model which is now being sought is that of the undeveloped tribal society which maintains the handicapped (who survive) in the community. It is true that in simpler societies they may be assigned a role which may be welcomed, feared, surrounded with religious mystery and taboo, or merely accepted and ignored. In Europe and North America we have seen attempts by society or by particular handicapped groups at assigning specific and separate roles—music or begging to the blind for example—and at more or less complete segregation in hospitals or asylums, at least for the most handicapped, coupled with the formerly familiar phenomenon of the deformed 'fool' at court and the 'village idiot' in the country. More recently, with the great development of segregated special education, sheltered employment and the like, and recognition (and survival) of different and usually more severely handicapped groups, there have been aspirations towards greater integration of the handicapped with the normal; but these aspirations have too often been frustrated by the very help provided and by the sheltered communities of school and work considered to be necessary.

The problem is a dual one—that of the adaptation of a handicapped child or adult to life in an unhandicapped world, and that of the community in adjusting to a handicapped minority in its midst, making allowances without sentimentality and accepting the handicapped as people with their own qualities and differences. Unfortunately, handicap does not necessarily awaken compassion and understanding in others, and few families with handicapped children are without experiences of humiliation, of indifference and downright unhelpfulness. Some handicaps, of course, are more easily accepted than others: blindness, for example, or physical handicap tend to evoke pity and helpfulness; physical deformity, severe mental handicap and very disturbed behaviour may provoke immediate rejection and fear. By and large, however, the general public, and children in particular, can only come to behave in a kindly but unsentimental way to the handicapped if they have the opportunity to learn to live with others who, although different, are accepted without stigma by the community.[15] This is the strongest argument for integrated community care for the handicapped.

Such an ideal is only realizable if it informs the thinking of all those concerned with the child and his family, and if every provision which is made is scrutinized to see how far it fits in ultimately with the aim of integrating the handicapped person into normal life. It involves hard decisions as to priorities in the use of resources—concerning, for example, levels of support necessary to maintain a child at home or to place him in an ordinary school, as compared with the cost of institutions or residential special schools; the provision of hostels for those who cannot live at home, or of small community homes for twenty to twenty-five children rather than large institutionalized units or hospitals; the use of peripatetic staff of all kinds to bring services to families, children and schools rather than children to treatment centres. It means, too, adaptations—sometimes costly—of the normal home and school environment to reduce the problems of the handicapped, the provision of clubs where handicapped and non-handicapped can meet and mix, holiday accommodation and many other arrangements to diminish the tendency of a handicap to emphasize abnormality.

At present, one of the principal problems for the family of a handicapped child is the fact that no one person, no one service, is responsible. Instead, they tend to be surrounded by specialists and services of different kinds, with differing competences (and degrees of ignorance about the others) and pre-occupations, often with differing views, and offering diagnoses, advice and prognostications which may be in conflict. Only too often it is the parents who have to attempt, unaided, to reconcile the claims and prescriptions which are made, and not infrequently they are either not fully informed, informed too late, or peremptorily told by an impersonal administration what is to happen to their child without consultation or discussion.[16]

We cannot go into detail here as to the specific services required,[17] but it is clear that education, health, social, vocational and leisure services are all necessary, and that at various points in a child's life, specialized units within particular services or involving a number of services will be required. Any handicapped child presents a complex of competing needs, and his presence deeply and continuously affects the lives of those about him, especially his immediate family. Hence, from the highest level of ministries of education, health, social security and employment down to the immediate local level, there is need for co-ordination and co-operation of a kind which brings the disciplines involved—psychology and child development, medicine, education, and social work—closely together and working in harmony. Generally, too, while parents and children must of necessity come into contact at different times with different specialists, they need some *one* person to whom, in doubt, difficulty or crisis, they can turn for advice and help, and who has the power and the knowledge both to inform them and to see that they get the service they need.

NOTES

1. Wall, W. D. *Constructive education for children.* Paris, Unesco/London, Harrap, 1975. Chapters six, eight and nine. (The first volume in the present series.)

2. For a discussion of the training of psychologists and teachers to deal with handicap, see: *Constructive education for adolescents,* chapters seven and eight. See also: Mittler, P., ed. *The psychological assessment of mental and physical handicaps.* London, Methuen, 1970.

3. A full treatment of normal adolescent development, its personal, familial and educational consequences, is given in Wall, W. D. *Constructive education for adolescents.* Paris, Unesco/ London, Harrap, 1977, the second volume in the present series.

4. If only to reassure them that in most cases there is little or no risk of giving birth to a handicapped child, parents who already have a handicapped child or with a family history of handicap, and the handicapped themselves, need sensitive genetic counselling. Even where the risk exists, it is practically never 100 per cent, although it can be as high as 1:2, but is not commonly greater than 5 to 10 per cent—for example, the chance of cleft palate in a couple with a familial history of the deformity is 3–4 per cent, rising to 9 per cent after the birth of two children. It is not sufficient for most intending parents to put it in these cold, statistical terms; time and discussion are essential to help them reach a wise decision.

5. In *The mill on the floss,* George Eliot gives a sensitive study of a handicapped adolescent (Philip) in his relations with the heroine.

6. See for example: Carlson, E. R. *Born that way.* Evesham, Arthur James, 1952; New York, John Day, 1968; Mallinson, V. *None can be called deformed.* London, Heinemann, 1956.

7. Eisenberg (Chairman's closing remarks) in Rutter, M., ed. op. cit., note 10, chapter 1.

8. Richman, N. Depression in mothers of pre-school children. *J. child psychol & psychiatr.* (Elmsford, N.Y., Association of Child Psychology & Psychiatry), vol. 17, no. 1, 1976.

9. See, for example, Chapter 6 of: Davie, R.; Butler, N.; Goldstein, H. op. cit., note 8, chapter 1.

10. Bronfenbrenner, U. *In:* Clarke, A. M. and Clarke, A. D. B., eds. *Early experience: myth and evidence.* London, Open Books, 1976.

11. Harrison, M.; Laxton, W. *Home start.* Leicester, Leicester Council of Voluntary Service, 1970; United Kingdom. Department of Education and Science. *Educational priority.* Vol. 4. London, H.M.S.O., 1975; Poulton, G. A.; James, T. *Preschool learning in the community.* London, Routledge & Kegan Paul, 1975.

12. See: Butler, N. R.; Bonham, D. G. *Perinatal mortality.* London, Livingstone, 1963; Butler, N. R.; Alberman, E. D. *Perinatal problems.* London, Livingstone, 1969; and especially: Davie, R.; Butler, N. R.; Goldstein, H. op. cit., note 8, chapter 2.

13. Masse, G. Les registres de risques et de l'enfance handicapée en Grande Bretagne: applications possibles en France. *Rev. fr. aff. soc.* (Paris, Ministère de la santé; Ministère du travail), 1970, vol. 24, no. 4, p. 3–22. Masse shows how the method, evolved in the United Kingdom (though by no means universally applied) could be adapted to the French social and medical services. See also: WHO Regional Office for Europe. *Working group on the early detection and treatment of handicapping defects in young children.* Copenhagen, WHO, 1968; and particularly: Alberman, E. D.; Goldstein, H. The 'at risk' register: a statistical evaluation. *Br. j. prev. & soc. med.* (London, British Medical Association), vol. 24, no. 3, 1970.

14. Wall, W. D. *Constructive education for adolescents.* op. cit., chapter 8, 'psychological services'.

15. Tizard, J. *Community services for the mentally handicapped.* London, O.U.P., 1964.

16. The first chapter of Younghusband, E. L., et al. *Living with handicap.* London, National Bureau for Co-operation in Child Care, 1970, presents an analysis of letters from over 400 parents about their experiences with a handicapped child and their encounters with the medical, social and educational services.

17. The matter is discussed in great detail in Younghusband, E. et al., op. cit. see above note 16, and, so far as France is concerned, in Mande R.; Masse N.; Manciaux, M. op. cit. References to services in other countries will be found in Special education. *Bulletin of the International Bureau of Education* (Geneva, IBE) no. 175/176, 1970.

Chapter four

The education of physically handicapped children

INTRODUCTION

The schools of a nation are necessarily normative but their avowed object is the education of all children. More and more, over the past decades, the education given in ordinary schools has been adapted to take account of individual differences among children and the consequent variety of needs presented even by a so-called average group. But this adaptation has not gone nearly far enough to meet the problems we now know to exist even among pupils considered to be normal. There is, moreover, a degree of deviation found in a proportion of children and adolescents—in ability to learn, in sensory equipment, in physical tolerance or in emotional development—which, with the best will in the world and the most skilful teaching, makes their education in an ordinary class difficult—at least without the risk of grave sacrifice of the interests either of the 'normal' children or of the deviants themselves.

The limits of such tolerance will depend partly upon the flexibility of the school or class organization, upon the rigidity or otherwise of the curricula, the size of the group, the availability of equipment, but most of all upon the skill, knowledge and training of the teachers. For example, a highly trained and experienced teacher can accept a considerable proportion of children with mild handicaps into a class of thirty or thirty-five; and such a teacher could certainly, with auxiliary help if necessary, so organize the activities of a group of ten children as to give them a sound education even though their ability ranged from the markedly subnormal to near genius, and though several of them had fairly severe physical or sensory handicaps.[1] On the other hand, one blind child or one child with a severe personality difficulty might either disorganize the work of a class of thirty to thirty-five pupils or himself be neglected, unless (and sometimes even if) auxiliary help is freely available in the classroom. Moreover, even a lavish provision of auxiliary help is only likely to be satisfactory if the school staff have the basic knowledge and training to cope with day-to-day problems, and if expert assistance is available from outside to meet times of crisis.

In the developing countries struggling to provide an effective primary education for all children, general provision for special needs even in special schools or classes is apt to be sketchy if it is made at all. It starts with the most obvious handicaps (e.g. blindness and deafness) and is often left to private or religious benevolence.[2] One should also remember that in countries where the health services, and particularly the ante-, peri- and post-natal maternity services, are not highly developed, and where nutritional standards are low, minor handicaps at least may be the norm among school children rather than the exception; and large numbers may suffer from sensory defect, motor and intellectual impairment due to birth injuries, to antenatal malnutrition or to crippling endemic diseases like trachoma. In such circumstances the problems of handicap present themselves in a different social and emotional context: primary prevention is a major and urgent problem; and secondary prevention, that is to say reduction or elimination of the personal and economic effects of severe handicapping conditions by means of education, rehabilitation and adequate social and vocational services, may seem inevitably a second priority. One tends to find too that, in those ordinary schools containing many children who, in more prosperous regions would be singled out for help, the teachers are the least well-trained to mitigate the effects of handicap on learning.

Convenience of medical and para-medical treatment and the heterogeneous nature of the difficulties of handicapped and delicate children have led in advanced education systems to many of them being sent to special schools and to a preponderance, at least for the severely handicapped, of hospital or boarding school provision. In some cases this may be unavoidable, particularly if the ordinary school system is neither alert to, nor equipped to cater for, the handicapped; but the grave disadvantages for the child himself should not be overlooked. A boarding school, for example, tends to cut him off for considerable periods from his family; and by the very grouping together of many handicapped children isolates them from the community. Furthermore, such children are likely to be fairly representative of the whole range of educational ability and age found in an ordinary school population; a group of some sixty or a hundred of them will thus have a great variety of special needs for which, in spite of smaller classes, the special school may not be able adequately to provide. The tradition that all or most of such children need an education with a predominantly manual or vocational content dies hard, yet among them are a proportion for whom a more academic and intellectual education is a necessity and who could, properly handled, later enter professions for which their disability constitutes no particular handicap. Even special day schools involve a considerable element of segregation and of labelling and may—because they are small—not be able to cater fully for the variety of their pupils' needs. The decision to segregate a physically handicapped child from his normal fellows and from his family is not to be lightly taken and certainly not principally upon grounds of administrative convenience. Much more could and should be done to integrate such children into ordinary schools and classes and, where this is not possible, to bring the special school or class into a close functional relationship with the ordinary education system of the district.[3]

MAJOR OR MINOR HANDICAP

It is important to distinguish between the large group of children with minor (and often undetected) handicaps and the very much smaller proportion of those with a severe physical or mental disability. For those who are very severely handicapped, separate and special educational provision may often be necessary—though perhaps not in as many cases as has hitherto been thought—but it is very expensive in material and human resources. Even in the relatively prosperous countries of North America and Europe, arrangements are not considered to be fully adequate, and in many countries certain needs are not met at all; some groups are excluded from the education system or not administratively recognized, and receive no education or one ill-adapted to them. Certainly in the developing countries, the services provided even for major groups like the blind and deaf are at best a token of concern, and provision for the more expensive kinds of secondary prevention is given a comparatively low priority.

The dramatic nature of gross handicap leads to early detection, and this has tended to concentrate attention on its physical and medical aspects at the expense of a more constructive, educational approach directed at making the best—personally, educationally and vocationally—of the individual's resources. Labelling by physical syndromes—blind, deaf, cerebrally palsied, epileptic and the like—may also lead to a categorization which is false and misleading for the ultimately more important purpose of developing each child educationally; and the very terms used suggest that the problems are more or less exclusively medical and physical. It is true that some handicapped children and adolescents will require medical treatment and rehabilitation of a major and continuing kind. More will require some form of continued medical supervision. But when physical treatment has done its utmost, and even with very severely physically handicapped children whose handicap has imposed deprivation or grossly impaired their ability to learn, we still have a child or adolescent whose primary emotional, social and intellectual needs remain those of all children. It is because any hope of a satisfactory life depends upon the child's ability to learn and to adjust that modern practice is beginning to put the primary responsibility for all handicapped children on the education system, and to insist on the importance of psychological and educational as well as medical supervision from birth.

Unless a handicap affects vision or hearing or critically important parts of the central nervous system (and even then by no means invariably), there may be little or no necessary or direct relationship between the severity or nature of the physical condition itself and the educational and personal difficulties to which it gives rise. We are dealing with a system of complex interaction of which a physical deformation, deficiency or weakness and its treatment is one element, but not necessarily the most important. The environment, the other resources of the individual, the kind of help and support he gets from home and school, play a critical and sometimes determinant part. Moreover, handicap is rarely simple or confined to one part or organ of the body. Even in very mild cases it tends to be multiple, and often no one defect is sufficiently predominant either to be singled out as a cause or to provide a useful guide to categorization for educational purposes.

Gross disabilities or defects—like blindness, deafness, motor impairment, major damage to the central nervous system, certain glandular or enzyme deficiencies or malfunctions—are usually detected in infancy. Such cases, however, are relatively infrequent compared to physically and physiologically much slighter impairments which may pass unnoticed in the early years and not be detected until a child matches up to his peers in school. What is still too frequent, and much commoner than the gross and apparent disability, is the child who presents a developing and pervasive learning difficulty, often social and motivational as well as strictly cognitive. Closer examination shows that this has developed as a consequence of a deficit or a constellation of sensory, physical and environmental handicaps, not in and by themselves of manifest and direct educational importance, and often so slight as to have escaped medical detection. In another important group of cases, there is a mild sensory defect (like impaired hearing) or a communication difficulty (mechanical or to do with a maturational lag or deviation), or a neurological impairment which has perhaps been treated medically so far as possible, but no steps have been taken to palliate the effects on the child's early learning or to meet the disturbances of behaviour, concentration or impulse inhibition to which it may lead. Such children are often thought to be mentally subnormal and/or malad-justed—and indeed may have become so because their educational needs have not been met soon enough. In other children, the problem may simply be one of lowered vitality or restricted activity. The child is not ill but persistently in poor physical condition. In many of these cases—because of the association of poor physical condition in the child with poverty or low educational and socio-economic status in the home—the deprivations and difficulties imposed by the handicap are grossly compounded by the environment.

In all such cases the physical condition of the child should be treated as far as possible, but it would be foolish to believe that this alone would put things straight. What is principally necessary is wise and understanding educational guidance from the earliest possible moment in his development, an adjustment of method and demand, at home and at school, to the child's capacities. This is not a matter of vague goodwill but involves a carefully devised programme based upon a clear understanding of how the various aspects of handicap and its treatment have played, and continue to play, a part in his difficulties—the effects upon him, for example, of lack of mobility in the early years, the language problems imposed by hearing loss, the consequences of repeated absence from school, of lack of opportunities for play or of restricted experi-ence. In developed and developing countries alike many such children will be—and rightly so—found in ordinary classes; it is here that they and many of their more evidently seriously handicapped fellows should be helped by the ordinary teacher, assisted where necessary by expert advice and auxiliary help. This has obvious implications, not only for the ways in which the primary and secondary schools of a country are organized, but for the training of all teachers—pre-school, primary and secondary—who need to know a great deal more than they know at present about human learning and the ways in which it may be impeded by handicap. It also implies that medical staff need sufficient training in the psychological and educational aspects of child development to enable them to appreciate the importance, at a very early age, of a much more educationally and psychologically oriented programme of primary prevention, diagnosis and rehabilitation.

Progress in these respects is hampered, as we have said earlier, by the assumption that medical and pseudo-medical classifications (most of which are descriptive rather than diagnostic) have a direct and linear relationship to the kinds of educational environments at home and at school needed by children with particular handicaps or potentialities. The worst effect of this is the almost automatic segregation of severely impaired children from their ordinary fellows and from each other by grouping them according to their major handicap in schools of different kinds, each supposedly specialized for a particular type of defect and its appropriate pedagogy. But there are pervasive secondary consequences. For example, where teachers are specially trained for work with the handicapped, there is a tendency to train them to concentrate upon a particular handicap and a particular stylized pedagogy. But the heterogeneity of any handicapped group calls for two capacities in those who educate them: a profound knowledge of the way normal human beings learn and develop; and a varied armoury of educational strategies from which to select those appropriate to the individual child. A teacher (or medical officer) trained specifically for one 'class' of handicap will overlook factors crucial to education and rehabilitation—many of them more important in cause and remedy than the factor covered by the familiar label.

CLASSIFICATION

A growing appreciation of the complexity of the educational needs of the handicapped has led to some increased flexibility both in the categories used for classification and in the kind of educational provision made. Most developed systems, however, still have a tradition of, and a heavy investment in, special schools and institutions to which pupils are allocated according to a primarily—even exclusively—medical diagnosis of the most important presenting handicap. This tradition is especially strong in the case of those groups which were the earliest to be recognized and which seem to have some sort of clearly definable educational need, requiring a special training on the part of their teachers: the blind and the deaf are examples. Immediately following the Second World War there was a strong tendency in Europe to increase the number of categories of children requiring special educational treatment (because of handicap) in separate schools or classes. For example, the Education Act of 1944 in the United Kingdom stated that all children have the right to education according to their age, ability and aptitude, and subsequent regulations established a great number of categories,[4] including maladjusted, delicate, children with speech defects, and so on. Subsequently, either by central action or by local effort, other categories have been added: cerebrally palsied: 'autistic'; even 'dyslexic';[5] and children who have suffered from the side effects of such drugs as thalidomide. And the pressure is to assign such children to schools specially conceived for them.

The wisdom of any such categorization, however widely defined, and of labelling in general, is being increasingly questioned.[6] There is a growing emphasis upon strictly educational criteria operationally defined, that is to say 'educational subnormality' or 'special educational need'. Such a descriptive label says nothing as to causes or categories, nor does it provide a pseudo or incomplete diagnosis. It permits the development of each child to be treated and planned for as an individual without a stereotyping label. The education authorities in an increasing number of countries are now required by law to discover all such children of school age and to make suitable provision for them. Moreover, in some countries parents have the right to bring their children, from the age of 2, to the attention of the education authorities if they believe them to be handicapped in any way, and to ask that adequate educational provision be made for them. In fact what seems to be happening generally as our understanding develops is that the somewhat simplistic medical model of a symptomatic diagnosis leading to a specific treatment is slowly changing in favour of an educational model which starts from where the child is, assays the positive aspects of the child's ability to learn and profit from what the school has to offer, and builds upon that. 'Diagnosis' is not a one-time judgement but a process over time; careful observation, psychological investigation and diagnostic teaching reveal individual patterns of learning. Handicap of whatever kind is seen for what it is: important mainly in terms of the impediment to learning which it may set up.[7] In many countries, even the very severely intellectually retarded—frequently categorized as 'ineducable' and mentally 'defective' in the past—are now regarded as a primary responsibility of educational rather than of medical authorities. They are no longer abandoned in hospitals without training or education, but helped much more to live in the community. Special schools and classes too are becoming less specialized by overt diagnostic categories and more concerned with general learning difficulty. The change is, however, slow and greatly impeded by conservative attitudes in teachers, medical practitioners and the general public which equate handicap or disability with disease.

Carried fully to its conclusion, the trend towards more constructive and educational concepts would stress that the range of learning ability which characterizes children in general will be found to be much the same for the handicapped with a very few necessary exceptions; and that there is a variety of conditions (of which physical handicap of one kind or the other is only one) which may make conventional education in an ordinary school difficult for any given child. It draws attention to the interrelation of educational, psychological, medical and social factors and to the need for a careful study of any child who fails to progress normally in his development. The central concern is with an individual's power to adjust, in the first place to education, and later to adult life; and with the pressures and facilitations which his environment provides and has provided in the past. Thus the study of a failing child becomes prospective rather than simply diagnostic, assessing his potentialities in relation to his home and educational environments, and leads to an attempt to modify both of them in positive ways. Correspondingly, too, it makes for greater caution in recommending special placements outside the normal system; it stresses flexibility and resourcefulness in ordinary educational provision. The assignment (when it has to be done) of a child to a particular type of special school or class is more cautious and more provisional; and a last resort. Moreover, if emphasis is placed upon differentiation of educational needs, upon improving and equipping the ordinary school and helping the teachers to cope, the procedures of legal certification—which have frequently come to mean total and irrevocable exclusion from the normal school system (and from normal life later on), and in the eyes of parents and the community a shameful stigma—can be abandoned.

This greater flexibility and greater child-centredness, with its emphasis on normality in dealing with the handicapped, proposes considerable, but no insuperable, practical problems for schools and teachers. It implies that, instead of accepting a relatively low level of educational, and later economic, success as an inevitable consequence of handicap, we should expect handicapped pupils to do as well as ordinary children of similar potential intellectual levels, and that, if they do not do so, the cause must be sought in the education given at home and in schools. This, in turn, demands that resources saved by diminishing the number of segregated placements be redeployed to assist ordinary schools and teachers to cope with handicap, and that appropriate remedial and supportive methods are developed. Moreover, it requires a positive effort to ensure that special schools, special classes, or indeed special arrangements within ordinary schools, do not lead to the development of closed, separated and, worse still, isolated communities or groups such as characterized special education in the inter-war years and earlier. On the other hand, once segregation by type of handicap is seen not to be of principal importance, special schools and classes where they are still essential can become less specialized and cater for a greater variety of educational needs. In the cases of certain handicaps which in the past have, because of their infrequency, been concentrated in (usually) residential schools, it becomes possible to find day school placements which are emotionally, socially and educationally more acceptable.

INTEGRATION

Most subnormal and physically or sensorially handicapped children will live in the community as adults. Hence, while they should not be put in destructive competition with their abler contemporaries during their school days, neither should they be segregated from them unless it is absolutely essential. Certain very low-grade defectives are probably best housed in institutions, but this is mainly in the interests of their families.[8] Some deeply handicapped, blind or deaf children require such a concentration of special methods that a separate boarding or day school seems necessary at least for a considerable time. But, before any step is taken to segregate the handicapped, especially in institutions, a most careful exploration should be made of other possibilities. For example, with specialized domestic and educational help some deeply defective or severely handicapped young children can be kept in their own home under the affectionate care of their mothers for at least the critical first part of childhood.[9] Where adequate social and economic assistance is available, this is not only sounder psychologically but may well be cheaper in practice. In large towns the provision of small day-care centres providing education and occupation for no more than some thirty to fifty profoundly and severely retarded children gives a respite to the family and provides for the child, under the skilled guidance of adequately trained teachers,[10] a social training as well as an adapted education. Similarly, day schools and classes for the physically handicapped—even if transport has to be arranged over considerable distances—are better than residential institutes. Even the dullest child is susceptible to affection and individual care; no institution can provide the same continuity of emotional stimulus as is provided by even a moderately successful home; and there is little doubt that the care and affection of a family provide the background for a genuine, if circumscribed, education for all, with the possible exception of the dangerously violent cases or the completely incapable idiots. What is important is that the family, and especially the mother, should be generously helped in what is after all a very difficult, exacting and emotionally exhausting task.

The blind and partially sighted, the deaf and hard-of-hearing, the severely physically handicapped and those children who, while not profoundly retarded, cannot learn normally in ordinary classes as they are usually organized—that is to say a few of the mildly and most of the moderately retarded—are at present usually placed in segregated special day schools. But it seems probable that for many more of the physically and sensorially handicapped and for the relatively high-grade and emotionally stable pupils among the mildly retarded, and certainly for the markedly dull, who often find themselves in special schools, a better solution is the special class, as fully integrated as possible into an ordinary school. Of course this has to be so handled that the needs of the handicapped neither unduly interfere with the smooth running of the rest of the school nor are unduly sacrificed to it.[11] Better still (though more difficult) is either to organize, staff and equip some ordinary classes so that they can cater for a wider range of ability and learning problems, or to withdraw handicapped pupils to specially staffed remedial groups for some of the curriculum (for example special language work with the deaf, braille for the blind, aspects of reading or mathematics for those who have marked difficulty with these subjects) and to integrate them with the whole class of normal children for others (for example music, singing, craftwork, drama and so on).[12] In this way some of the social stigma which still clings to abnormalities of all kinds may be avoided, and handicapped and normal children be brought into close and understanding contact with each other instead of being segregated. It has the further advantage of allowing those members of the teaching staff specialized for the education of the handicapped to maintain easy contact with the needs and capacities of normal pupils.

Many handicapped children, as we have seen, have complicated constellations of difficulties and handicaps; frequently they cannot conform to the rhythm of the normal school day, need special physical treatment, speech training or psychological help. Some are markedly unstable and require constant supervision; others live in remote rural districts. Children of this kind certainly constitute an administrative difficulty; but there seems little reason—except rather unimaginative preconceptions and adherence to traditional arrangements—why the necessary additional services, para-medical and psychological, should not be organized on a peripatetic basis in very many more circumstances than at present and be brought to children in their schools as an alternative to residential segregation. This is, of course, easier in large urban centres; in sparsely populated rural areas there seems no real reason why such children should not be concentrated in small numbers in some ordinary schools, living during the week in foster homes, and returning home at the weekends—as has been done with deaf children in New Zealand.

Where boarding accommodation is the only practicable solution, the schools should have not only a qualified educational staff but sufficient domestic and auxiliary staff to assure a genuinely personal and homelike care. Such schools (contrary to much current practice) should—for the sake of both staff and children—be situated near enough to a real community, a small town or village, so that pupils and staff may live in contact with normal life and not become isolated. So too the school should make every effort to keep in close touch with the child's family, and as far as is practicable the child should return home for holidays.

PRE-SCHOOL EDUCATION

A word should be said about pre-school education for the handicapped. In the majority of countries the compulsory period of education does not begin before the age of 6 and in many before the age of 7. Most countries which have arrangements for special education at the primary level also provide pre-school facilities usually at least for the blind and the deaf, and usually from the age of 3.

Very often this pre-school provision, where it exists, consists of a special school or an institution for the blind or deaf, or a special unit in a hospital or medical care centre, though countries like Bulgaria, Czechoslovakia, Sweden and the U.S.S.R. have special kindergartens. A growing practice, and one to be commended, is the provision of special classes in ordinary nursery schools or, best of all, the full integration of young handicapped into the nursery school with appropriate remedial support of all kinds. In addition, as in countries like the Philippines, Saudi Arabia and Sweden, home guidance services are of great value to complement the work of the nursery school or even to take its place.

It is obvious that the earlier steps can be taken to minimize the intellectual, social and emotional effects of a handicap the better; but if pre-school provision for the handicapped is considered merely or mainly as serving a social or custodial function, it may well be robbed of most of its potential value. We now know the importance and value, for example, of early help to the deaf in the acquisition of speech. It seems likely that many other handicaps require a pre-school programme with clear cognitive and instrumental aims. Attendance at a nursery school, therefore, for any handicapped child should be regarded as a period of progressive educational observation, of deliberate attempts to supplement or compensate for deficiencies and defects, and of discriminating educational diagnosis.

It is equally important that such pre-school institutions as exist should work with the parents of handicapped children, both while they are in school and before they come. The qualified pre-school educator can be expected to know a great deal about normal development of young children by training and experience, and from this background help parents of the handicapped to normalize the life of their child.

SECONDARY EDUCATION

At the other end of the compulsory period, it is noticeable that, even if one disregards those who are intellectually handicapped to a considerable degree (whether otherwise handicapped or not), the handicapped are present in ordinary secondary education, if at all, in woefully small numbers; and, *a fortiori*, fewer still in higher education.[13] This is partly because in such well-established areas as the domain of the blind or deaf, special secondary schools already exist outside the ordinary systems; partly, it is because such post-primary education as exists for the handicapped follows the traditional belief that their future occupations will tend to be subaltern and mainly manual; and partly because, once a child is in a special system, it is difficult for him to get out, particularly where the entry requirements to ordinary secondary education are rigid. Even then, those who do accede to academic and other specialized forms of secondary education may well find the task of maintaining themselves within it very difficult, because of the multiplicity of teachers, problems of mobility and the physical size of the schools themselves. None of these is a problem which with skill and sympathy cannot be solved and it is reasonable to suppose that many more handicapped adolescents could profit from an academically exacting secondary education than are allowed to do so at present.

Many countries do, however, consider it valuable to prolong compulsory education, for at least a year beyond the general legal limit and in some for longer—for example, two years in some states of the United States of America, and for the mentally handicapped in Sweden up to the age of 21 or 23 if necessary.[14]

EDUCATION OF THE DULL-NORMAL AND MILDLY SUBNORMAL

As can be seen from the Table 1 on page 23, intellectually retarded children of all groups amount to about 2·5 per cent of the population of school age. Few European countries make full provision for the whole of this group, and most have special schools or classes for little more than half of those who need it. The dull-normal, who are four or five times as numerous[15] as the subnormal, are scarcely anywhere recognized as a considerable group for whom modification of the customary standards and ordinary teaching methods may be necessary. Where some more-or-less adequate provision is made, only too often no distinction is drawn between them and those whose relative educational failure is due to causes other than an apparently inferior educable capacity. In addition, there are many children who are labelled and classified in other handicapped groups—physically handicapped, delicate, speech defective, sensorially handicapped—but who are nonetheless also intellectually retarded, dull or simply educationally subnormal.

For such children (otherwise handicapped or not) an education which makes no allowance for their more limited functional ability or their particular educational difficulties, especially in a school system which has a rigid system of annual promotion by attainment,[16] tends to be a period of continued failure. Teachers, parents and children may withdraw and lower their aspirations. On the other hand, children may find themselves in a situation of effort made without success and—rather sooner than later—abandoned as useless, of disappointment to themselves, and of reproach from their teachers and parents. Such a mismatch between the individual's resources and the demands made by the environment, particularly that of the school with its apparently clear-cut but still arbitrary standards, inevitably leads to stress and to a general maladjustment, at least while it lasts. Many children, of course, survive this stress or adjust to it in the primary school at the cost of a considerable general underfunctioning; they do not achieve in school even the limited progress of which they are capable. Not a few are more permanently and severely damaged; and among them are those who develop behaviour and personality problems consequential upon their failure, or whose failure is intensified by their disturbance. For all such children, the transition to secondary education is likely to be difficult; nor are they well equipped to confront the identity crisis and the range of personal, social, vocational and moral choices which puberty and adolescence bring. As we have seen earlier, many handicapped children of good intellectual ability are not offered the possibility of the more selective or more vocationally appropriate forms of secondary education. Some become aggressive and difficult, even delinquent. It is not strange either that in later life some of them lapse into semi- or total illiteracy, become increasingly unstable or take refuge in their handicap; or that a general inefficiency leads many of them to swell the ranks of the unemployed and unemployable, becoming a costly social liability instead of contributing, as well they might, to society and leading lives adjusted to and making the most of their capacities.[17]

PESSIMISM

Much of our pedagogy of handicapped, intellectually retarded and dull children is dominated by doubtless good-hearted but still fundamentally pessimistic attitudes. Our administrative categorizations, although they have become more subtle and flexible in the past decades, still tend to sanction what is, rather than indicate what might be. This has become all the more serious since research is making us increasingly aware that any label we use covers a great variety of causes, function and outlook; and that children with learning difficulties are, if anything, more varied than others. Tacitly, and sometimes openly, such labels are interpreted to imply a fixed, genetically or physically limited, level of ability to learn and a relative constancy over time of the initial measure of learning capacity. As a consequence, many institutions and their staff accept for all their pupils a level of functioning below what might be achieved were the expectations of both child and teacher somewhat higher. Institutions and special schools for the handicapped of all kinds are too often content with a reasonable degree of socialization, the formation of habits useful in the immediate environment, and a preparation for entry into some heavily protected form of adult life and work.

In itself, of course, such minimal socialization and limited independence would be no mean result for very many of the more severely physically and intellectually handicapped children and adolescents who, in other circumstances, might easily have become entirely institutionalized, maladjusted, delinquent or subject to exploitation in various ways. But many mildly retarded children (and their teachers) adopt a level of aspiration which excludes, for example, an attainable level of simple functional literacy and skill in the discharge of relatively easy but still somewhat complex tasks involving concrete reasoning. It is often forgotten that, though the rate of many children's learning may be markedly slower than the average, the learning itself may well reach nearly to the range of the normal—if a longer time for learning, practice and consolidation is allowed. But even a prolongation of schooling and educational care, an advantage in itself, tends to fail or even be counter productive unless the school constructs a special programme for such children with cognitive and other goals similar (though of course adapted) to those expected for average children and embodying an optimistic view of their capacities.

EXPECTATIONS AND SELF-IMAGE

So too the dull-normal, whether otherwise handicapped or not, and whether in special classes or ordinary schools, are often regarded as merely stupid for primarily genetic reasons; they are 'born that way' and destined always to be inferior, a kind of second-class citizen—even when it is manifest that their dullness is the product of a poor environment or a secondary consequence of another handicap. For some it may indeed seem hopeless to expect even slight improvement, but it is never safe to accept a deterministic view of learning ability. A curriculum and method emphasizing goals which, although realistically attainable, imply a confidence in the pupils' ability to achieve progressively more (rather than some sort of segregated simplification which marks their difference and inferiority) is likely to bring them to a higher level of functioning. To a considerable extent the problem is that of the image of himself which the child builds up bit by bit from comparisons with others, from his successes and failures, and from what he perceives that teachers and parents believe about him. If a school system uniquely accentuates competitive intellectual performance, particularly in such areas as reading and arithmetic, it will make apparent to all children certain exclusive criteria of success and failure, by which some are bound to fail disastrously. Very soon, quite young children establish a 'pecking order' among themselves in terms of whatever goals the teacher is seen to approve; any discrepancy between what the teacher appears to expect and what the child can reasonably hope to succeed in doing can become painful and negative in its feedback to the child's idea of himself. On the other hand, if the teacher manifestly reduces his expectations for some, particularly if in doing so he appears to reject the dull or handicapped—or perhaps, what is worse, sentimentalize them—there is the risk that the child will conform to this idea of himself. This problem of adjusting expectations to the real possibilities of individual pupils, of setting up for any group a manifestly acceptable difference and variety in educational goals, is perhaps the most crucial, especially from the mental health point of view, in all education; it is particularly critical in the education of handicapped pupils of all kinds.

If adequate and positive goal-setting is to be achieved it must be recognized that the mildly retarded and the dull, even if their cognitive disabilities are a consequence of another handicap, have special needs and make special demands upon the teacher's skill. Their most marked and general disability tends to be in the verbal field and, later, in all those operations which require abstract reasoning. Hence, in varying degrees according to progressive assessment of their potentialities and to a continued and well-informed study of their progress, the curriculum should be based upon concrete reasoning, practical work, the development of manual skills, and upon increasing social independence.

CURRICULUM

But it perhaps still needs to be emphasized that the curriculum and methods appropriate to the dull-normal, and still more to the mildly retarded, are not to be regarded either as narrowly vocational or as a diluted version of the programme for average or superior children.[18] A precocious vocational training, for example, which is still considered in some education systems as appropriate for the handicapped generally, neglects both the child's over-all needs and the facts of industrial employment. A handicapped child who is taught a trade and nothing else, particularly if he is subnormal or dull, may become proficient in its mechanical aspects but be unable to adapt himself to change.

With a variation in organization or machinery, he finds himself unemployable without a further lengthy period of re-training.

In the absence of specific disabilities, all the dull and most of the mildly retarded (handicapped or not) can learn to read sufficiently to make use of notices, newspapers and to enjoy simple books. The giving and receiving of change, the management of a family budget, calculations of wages, simple additions and subtractions of money, elementary calculations of space and volume such as are required in some semi-skilled and unskilled jobs, are within the range of all but the least able,[19] if they are taught concretely, slowly and with plenty of well-motivated practice in situations as near to real life as possible. While many, if not most, of such children, whether as adolescents or adults, are unlikely to grasp the advanced abstract conceptions or to form the generalized moral notions which lie behind discriminating ethical or social judgement and behaviour, the mildly retarded can understand notions of right and wrong, gain an elementary grasp of civic and political responsibility, to know their duties and rights as citizens, and be taught how to use the social and administrative machinery of their community, which exists to help and protect them. Moreover, most of the retarded and all the dull are capable of enjoying some at least of the more purely cultural aspects of their education—music, art, dancing and acting, for example—as well as of receiving a training which enables them to satisfy creative urges through concrete expression in wood, metal, leather and other materials. Only when such children have truly been educated as far as possible for the life which they will have to live as individual human beings is it legitimate to concentrate upon a purely vocational training; and even this should be much more than the inculcation of useful skills. Such children need skilled vocational guidance to make the best use of their capacities and a continued friendly supervision to integrate them into a working life which is stable and satisfying, and protected from exploitation or corruption.[20]

The needs of the dull and the retarded cannot easily be met if they are educated in large classes. But as has been stressed earlier, this does not necessarily imply segregation from the ordinary class. A re-deployment of resources of teachers, space and equipment would make possible classes in ordinary schools able to cater for a very much wider range of ability than is customary at present—particularly if the attitudes of teachers towards intellectual success and the artificial exigencies of centrally imposed curricula and standards were changed; and if, for example, two teachers with auxiliary help catered for a heterogeneous group of pupils learning individually or in small groups—heterogeneous or homogeneous as appropriate to the task in hand. Where, as is usually the case at present, special classes or schools are thought to be the answer for the mildly handicapped, the dull and the more able of the retarded, the maximum class size seems to be twenty pupils with one specially trained teacher. Even then the success of the group depends upon a careful selection of the children so that they are relatively stable emotionally and free from complicating difficulties. For those whose level of intelligence is lower—that is for most of the moderately retarded, or those whose subnormality is complicated by physical and particularly by neurological handicaps, by emotional disturbance or by specific psycho-physical defects—the groups should be smaller, the methods more individualized[21] and the contact between teacher and pupil even closer and more continuous. The programme should be so arranged that the teacher has the time and the energy to come intimately to understand each pupil, and, preferably, he or she should remain with the group for considerably more than a year, taking within his province not merely their education in the narrow sense of intellectual and physical skills but their whole social development.

EDUCATIONAL BACKWARDNESS OF THE HANDICAPPED

We have concentrated so far on those of the handicapped of all kinds who, for whatever cause, appear to be dull or intellectually retarded, many of whom need special pedagogical techniques to help them surmount their handicap. But, as we have seen, there are many in the mildly and severely physically handicapped groups whose ability to learn is initially, at least, probably no different from that of an average child—children with a motor handicap which is the result of accident or disease, some epileptics, asthmatics, spina bifida children and children with heart disease or other anomaly, and so on. Only too many of such children, even among the most intelligent, become educationally backward and emotionally disturbed, not as a direct result of their handicap, but as a consequence of the interference it causes with normal development and schooling. Such children tend to be absent from school more frequently than others, pass periods in hospitals or sanatoria, undergo painful treatments and suffer many restrictions of movement or experience; they become painfully aware of their difference from others and may believe themselves to be mocked, rejected or even punished because of their handicap.

With all forms of handicap, a major factor in planning help is the level of the child's learning ability.[22] Roughly speaking, the greater the degree of handicap, the higher must be the child's general ability in order to overcome the obstacles which his disability interposes in his educational development. To a considerable extent this is also true for those forms of physical treatment and re-education which depend upon intelligent co-operation. It has, for example, been found that those markedly or severely handicapped, cerebrally palsied children whose I.Q. is considerably below 80 do not always respond well to physiotherapy, speech therapy or special education as at present developed. On the other hand, schools which specialize in the education of those children who are not only blind but physically and mentally handicapped to so severe a degree as to have been considered ineducable have had a striking success in training such children to be physically independent, personally and socially well adjusted and, in a few cases, in developing something more than the rudiments of formal education.[23] A proportion of the pupils of such schools do become at least partially self-supporting, although they belong to a group for which hitherto little could be done.

Examples like these, and the apparent miracles wrought by the devotion, intuition and skill of teachers who undertake 'hopeless' cases of multiply handicapped children, draw attention to two things of great importance to the mental health of the community. A handicapped person may become not only an economic and social liability, both as a child and as an adult, but also the focus of severe emotional disturbance in his own family. In many of these latter cases, the only solution still proposed is that of removing the child completely from his own home and placing him in an institution. Indeed, the suggestion is still sometimes heard (and sometimes followed) that severely subnormal children should be separated from their mothers immediately after birth and institutionalized. It is, however, by no means sure that the mental health of the family or of the community is best served by shutting from sight even the most severely handicapped persons. Where adequate social, medical and educational services are available to help the family in its task, where from the earliest stages informed measures are taken to prevent psychological disturbance either in the child or in his family, and to promote the progressive social adaptation of the handicapped, many even of the most severe cases can continue to live, ultimately at far less social cost, with their parents or at least in the community with foster parents or in hostels; and some can gain a partial independence. The second important point to re-emphasize is that, whereas the primary prevention of many handicapping conditions is largely a matter for the health services, the control of the personal and social consequences of a handicap from the earliest stages demands wise psychological, educational and social guidance, and involves, sooner or later, many services. What is needed is a system of continuous educational and personal support to the parents and to the child himself, which will see to it that continuity is maintained and that gaps which occur are filled. The education and development of a handicapped child need careful and systematic planning in relation to parents and school. Someone prepared to maintain contact with child and family in a guidance role over a lengthy period should step in to help when things appear to be going wrong.

THE ROLE OF THE TEACHER

It is manifestly unrealistic and probably undesirable on general grounds to expect to meet a problem, even that involved with the relatively small number of cases of severe and moderate handicap, by increasing the number of places in segregated special schools or even by creating large numbers of special classes of various types, either grouped together in a single comprehensive unit or attached to ordinary schools.[24] Equally, it seems to be true from the French and British experience that many more even of these quite severely handicapped children could profit from a high quality of educational provision if it were available. An economically more viable and, for very many children, an educationally more acceptable approach is the following. Instead of simply putting them into ordinary schools and hoping for the best, special arrangements of all kinds are made so that the regular class teacher or the teacher of a special class integrated in an ordinary primary or secondary school can give the extra help and support to the handicapped pupil, and to his family, necessary to maintain his progress. This could be done on a much larger scale than at present if a number of conditions were fulfilled. The first and most obvious concerns the skills of the teacher. Since the problem of handicap is so pervasive, all teachers in their initial and in-service training should be made fully aware of the main kinds of handicap, the disadvantages they may inflict on a child and the principal means of meeting the exceptional child's needs. In particular, teachers need help in discriminating between an uncomplicated, even if severe, physical handicap and the kinds of learning and concentration difficulties frequently associated with neurological damage, or the effects upon a child of different styles of upbringing in the pre-school period. The main effort, therefore, in such training should not be on handicap *per se* but upon how human beings learn and on the ways in which education can capitalize on what a child *can* do and, if necessary, compensate for any experience and learning of which the handicap may deprive him.[25] In addition, many more teachers than at present should have advanced training, either generally for most kinds of handicap or for specialized groups, of which the most important, certainly numerically, is general educational subnormality; these teachers should be trained for and appointed to the ordinary school system to give general advice and support to their colleagues in a number of schools, as well as in special schools and classes.[26]

Since the presence of at least some kinds of handicapped pupils in an ordinary class may present considerable problems if their needs are to be met to a satisfactory degree, auxiliary teaching and non-teaching staff could be of great service, particularly as this would permit individual attention and the kind of close personal contact which remedial work requires in order to be fully effective. The schools, too, may need to be adapted somewhat—for example by the provision of ramps and lifts—to allow mobility to the physically handicapped and to provide facilities for such groups as the partially sighted or hard-of-hearing. And the rest of the school staff, as well as the pupils, should have some preparation to be able to accept children with special needs and often disfiguring handicaps. Finally, it should be stressed that adequate services of psychological and medical diagnosis and treatment, and of expert psychological, social and educational support for the teacher, child and family are necessary throughout school life and into at least the early years of employment.

NOTES

1. See, for example: Berg, K. H. *Verhaltensgrundformen bei Hilfsschülern*. Berlin-Charlottenburg, Carl Marhold Verlagsbuchhandlung, 1964.
2. A good example is Saudi Arabia where the first school (evenings only at first) for the blind was opened in 1958; two more followed in 1962 and a third in 1963. The first school for the deaf began in 1963 and for the mentally retarded in 1968. Saudi Arabia, Ministry of Education. *The story of special education*. Riyadh, n.d. (?1970) [Mimeo.] See also: Malin, A. J. The role of education for the mentally retarded. *In: Children's annual*. New Delhi, 1970; and Commonwealth Secretariat (United Kingdom). *Directory of special educational provision for handicapped children in developing Commonwealth countries*. London, 1971. Provision for handicapped groups made by private bodies outside the state system

often has the effect of cutting such children and their teachers off completely from the normal education system, and of installing a model which is economically unattainable and may be undesirable.

3. The expert working party called together by the National Children's Bureau (United Kingdom) lists thirteen different kinds of educational provision for the handicapped (Younghusband, E. L., et al. *Living with handicap*. London, National Bureau for Co-operation in Child Care, 1970). These range from full-time residential special schools to resource centres in ordinary schools, home teaching, and residential hostels enabling handicapped children to attend ordinary day schools and providing tutorial help in the evenings.

4. See, for example: United Kingdom, Ministry of Education. *Special educational treatment*. London, His Majesty's Stationery Office, 1946. Pamphlet no. 5. In 1899 permission was given to school authorities to provide education for physically defective, mentally defective and epileptic children in addition to the blind and the deaf. Six more categories were added in 1945: maladjusted; delicate; diabetic; speech defective; partially deaf; and partially sighted. See also: Jackson, S. *Special education in England and Wales*. Oxford, Oxford University Press, 1966; Parent, P.; Gonnet, C. *Les écoliers inadaptés*. Paris, Presses Universitaires de France, 1965; Meiev, H., ed. *Die Sonderschulen in der Stadt Zürich*. Zurich, Schulamt der Stadt Zürich, n.d. (?1965); Laycock, S. R. *Special education in Canada*. Toronto, Gage, 1963. A more recent report is by the Working Party of the National Children's Bureau cited above, note 3. It proposes a ten-fold classification: visual handicap; hearing impediment; physical handicap; speech and language disorder; specific learning disorder; intellectual handicap; emotional handicap; severe personality disorder; severe environmental handicap; severe multi-handicap. They stress that some form of categorization is necessary, chiefly for those concerned with planning and providing for special education, but that categories are not mutually exclusive, do not need to be rigidly defined, and do not have to differentiate all varieties of disability or to specify the varieties of special education. They suggest, moreover, that the categories should be reformulated from time to time in the light of experience and research. This they insist is more than changing labels; it involves a rethinking of the nature of special educational needs.

5. A good example of an incantatory but, in fact, purely descriptive label meaning simply that children have difficulty in reading. One could add 'dyscalculic' and 'dysorthographic' for good measure.

6. See: Hobbs, N., ed. op. cit., note 67, chapter 2.

7. See: Wall, W. D. Handicap and social casualties—review article. *J. moral educ.* (Windsor, National Foundation for Educational Research in England and Wales), vol. 4, no. 3, 1975.

8. In any decision affecting the education, care and treatment of a child, it seems important to reach a decision based upon the best interests of the family group of which he or she is part—rather than uniquely of the child.

9. See Chapter 2, page 18 and note 8. Tizard and Grad found that the social competence of intellectually retarded children and adolescents living with their families was considerably superior to that of the institutionalized group.

10. In some countries, centres of this type are still provided not by the education, but by the health or social security authorities; and the staff consequently do not form part of the education service, having different (and unfortunately usually inferior) training, status and salary. They tend to be custodial and occupational. Modern practice is more and more to bring such children within the ambit of educational provision and to ensure that those who care for them are trained specially to provide a stimulating programme along the lines of an enlightened nursery school. See chapter 2, note 6 and: Tizard, J. op. cit., note 15, chapter 3; and Williams, P.; Gruber, E. op. cit., note 17, chapter 2.

11. As is being done with great success in many of the *classes de perfectionnement annexées aux écoles primaires* in France, the 'advancement classes' in Israel, and elsewhere in an increasing number of places, such as the city of Leicester in the United Kingdom. The same thing is done at the secondary level in France, but this time with groups of classes (ninety pupils) for slightly mentally handicapped attached to the Collèges d'enseignement secondaire providing general education and occupational training. (See the Unesco study cited in note 72, chapter 2.)

12. Zmdel, H. *Probleme der schulischen Bildung und Erziehung des Geistesschwachen*. Bern, Hans Huber, 1965. This indicates ways of adapting education in ordinary classes to the needs of mentally handicapped pupils. Israel, Sweden and France have adjustment classes in ordinary schools, intended in principle to be for a short period and leading to rapid reintegration in an ordinary class. Children attend the ordinary class for part of the time throughout. (See Unesco study cited in note 72, chapter 2.)

13. Unesco. op. cit., note 72, chapter 2.

14. Ibid.

15. In a country with a population of some 40 to 50 millions one would expect at least half-a-million of such children between the ages of 7 and 14.

16. Promotion by age may, in a different way, be equally unfortunate. It means that the dull or handicapped child has not had time to learn at his own pace and is put into a new class to tackle new work before he has time to consolidate the old.

17. A much fuller treatment of grade repetition, failure in the primary stage of education, social and cultural disadvantage is given in Vol. I of this work, *Constructive education for children*. Chapter eleven, section B: 'Failure to learn'.

18. See: O'Connor, N.; Tizard, J. op. cit., note 15, chapter 2; Williams, P.; Gruber, E. op. cit., note 17, chapter 2.

19. Tansley, A. E.; Gulliford, R. *The education of slow learning children*. London, Routledge & Kegan Paul, 1960.

20. Marshall, A. *The abilities and attainments of children leaving junior training centres*. London, National Association for Mental Health, 1967; Baranyay, E. P. *The mentally handicapped adolescent: the Slough Project of the National Society for Mentally Handicapped Children*. Oxford, Pergamon, 1971.

21. It is here that programmed learning and even simple forms of teaching machines may be of considerable help if the programmes are carefully designed and based upon a clear diagnosis of needs. See: Klauer, K. J. *Programmierter Unterricht in Sonderschulen*. Berlin-Charlottenburg, Carl Marhold Verlagsbuchhandlung, 1964.

22. We are here in a difficulty since the development of general learning ability may be (in fact nearly always is to some extent) inhibited by the handicap and the effects are likely to be cumulative. Obviously two things are implied: first, that early detection of handicap and the institution of a remedial programme concerned to compensate the child for the deprivations of stimulus imposed by his disability enormously increase his chances; and second, that in assessing the ability of handicapped children, one is concerned with a very delicate qualitative as well as quantitative diagnosis of intellectual functioning. One must, for example, be aware of the possibility of marginal brain damage, of disturbance of visuo-spatial analysis, of sequencing difficulties and of dysfunctions of the central nervous system affecting speech.

23. Condover Hall Special School for the Multihandicapped Blind, Condover, Shrewsbury, Shropshire, England. The majority of the children of this school are below I.Q. 60, and a number are more or less severely crippled, though mobile. All have been placed there because they have been considered unsuitable for other forms of special education. The school has a special unit devoted to the deaf-blind.

24. *A fortiori*, in developing countries a probably much greater prevalence of handicaps dictates that the even scarcer resources should in the main go to the improvement of remedial and other special services in the ordinary schools rather than exclusively to the extension of special education—often in relatively expensive residential schools.

25. Akira Morishima (Japan) reports the case of Yoshihiko Yamamoto, a hydrocephalic boy whose highest tested I.Q. was 47 and who had great problems in the general verbal-educational area. His teacher encouraged him to keep a picture diary. At 26, Yoshihiko is a good artist who has won prizes for his work. Cited in: *New behaviour* (London), 26 June 1975, p. 438, from *Psychology today* (New York), vol. 9, p. 72.

26. More than half the physically handicapped children in Denmark and Sweden attend ordinary schools as the result of a clear policy of providing remedial teaching, transport, technical aids and personal assistance where necessary. Alternatively, there may be a special class in an ordinary school with hostel accommodation. In Denmark, by 1970, 51 per cent of the

physically handicapped were in ordinary classes, and a further 16·5 per cent in special classes in ordinary schools. Anderson, E. *Making ordinary schools special*. London, College of Special Education, 1971. See also: Haskell, S. H.; Anderson, Elizabeth Marion. Physically handicapped children: special or normal schooling? *Slow learning child* (Brisbane, Fred and Eleanor Schonell Educational Research Centre), vol. 16, no. 3, 1971.

Chapter five

Maladjusted and delinquent children and adolescents

Physically or sensorially handicapped and intellectually retarded children find adjustment to the normal world made difficult by particular—and usually noticeable—physical and mental limitations and, as we have seen, a higher than average proportion of them have severe or moderate personality and behavioural problems. School surveys show that there is also a group of children apparently physically and intellectually normal who, perhaps because of inherent anomalies of temperament, marked emotional instability or abnormal strength or weakness in one or other of the fundamental psychological drives, are handicapped to the extent that their personal development, even under favourable conditions and often from an early age, is recognizably deviant if not pathological. In addition, there are some who have central nervous system damage or other organic pathology, the main or only apparent symptoms of which are emotional or behavioural—for example the unstable post-encephalitic, certain of the epileptic, some children with cerebral tumours, children in whom a cerebral lesion gives rise to excessive activity, and the like—and a few psychotic children or children with a constellation of peculiarities which suggest imminent psychosis—depressive, manic or schizoid. Taken together, however, these children form only a fractional part[1] of those who, temporarily or permanently, show signs of maladjustment in the school period, or whose marked anomalies of emotional growth in adolescence are reflected in delinquency, in scholastic or vocational failure, or in marked deviations of personality development.

The classification of maladjustment, or even anything approaching a precise definition of what we mean by the word, is difficult—much more so than other forms of handicap. Many attempts have been made, all of them open to objections.[2] However elaborate the scheme,[3] very many children do not fit neatly into the categories because of the heterogeneity of their symptoms, the lack of clear relationship between apparent causes and apparent effects, and the way the expression of some sort of emotional disturbance varies with age and with circumstances. Probably the most useful categorization is the simplest: a broad distinction between conduct or behaviour problems on the one hand and personality problems on the other. Behaviour disorders suggest that the individual is more 'extroverted', may be aggressive or anti-social; and personality disorders suggest more 'neurotic' or 'emotional' disturbance, more introversion, inhibition and unhappiness. Again, however, it should be remarked that even such broad categories overlap, and are very far from being precisely definable.

CAUSES

It is possible that there are some situations which, without prior distortion of development, can dramatically give rise to maladjustment and neurosis. The sudden death of a beloved parent, the birth of a younger brother or sister, a scene of adult violence, may, supervening at a critical moment in psychological growth and without adequate interpretation to the child, provoke serious emotional disturbance which becomes apparent immediately and has reverberations subsequently. Whether in fact such a shock brings about a continuing maladjustment depends, however, to a considerable extent upon the reactions of other important figures—parents, older children, teachers—to the child's behaviour: it is an interactive process, stamping in some responses and eliminating others. Demands made upon a child to adjust may be too great either for his level of maturity or for his emotional force at that time, and instead of moving forward to a new and acceptable integration of behaviour, he may revert and remain fixed at an earlier level, or develop immediately successful but ultimately maladjusted coping techniques.

In any situation of difficulty or shock, the temptation is to retreat to a previously successful form of behaviour, and normal development in fact shows a series of advances and retreats, much like the waves of a rising tide. The important thing is that new and adaptative integrations should predominate and become steadily prepotent. The range of individual variation in adaptability is immense; what might be seriously damaging for one child leaves another more or less unruffled. Individual susceptibility to emotional shock is markedly influenced by constitutional factors, by all that has happened from the moment of birth, by the immediate situation, by the interpretation which the child comes to put upon it and by the sensitivity, insight and skill of important adults in the environment.

It is therefore rarely possible in any given case to trace the source of maladjustment to any one incident; though a particular happening in a child's life (for example entry to school) may well have been the precipitating cause, or, unassimilated and unexplained, may have given rise to a series of fears, attitudes and expectations, which later develop into a neurosis or into a behaviour or attitudinal deviation. Most usually, maladjustment grows slowly over time, resulting in a progressively more noticeable disequilibrium between the resources of an individual and the demands of his society. In all such cases the reaction of the individual begins by being normal and the abnormality is in the environment—that is, either the environment is frankly unsatisfactory and does not provide what a child needs for growth, or it is unsatisfactory for him and makes demands which his stage of growth does not enable him to meet.[4] An example of the first situation is that of continuing parental friction—a classic 'cause' of maladjustment—in which the child's security is assailed by the spectacle of open disunity between his parents, by a painful division of loyalties, and by the fantasy or real fear that they may kill each other. An example of the second is where the parents unite—very often lovingly—to exact standards of behaviour, manners at table, quietness in the house or tidiness, for example, which are quite beyond the child's power to accomplish. That in the one case the child should become anxious and endeavour to reinforce his security by clinging to his mother or should become openly aggressive towards others at school, and in the other should show lack of self-confidence, be obsessionally conformist or become aggressive and 'naughty', is perfectly normal. If, however, the situation provoking such reactions continues, the conflict may intensify and become interiorized as a permanent part of the child's whole unconscious life, thereby affecting his personality. He learns to cope in various ways, making adjustments which reduce the immediate tension, but which—even when the provoking situation no longer exists—colour his subsequent emotional life and operate as a factor in determining his style of adjustment to future challenges.

In effect, what this means is that much maladjustment is a disorganized form of learning. Child and parent appear to be engaged in a dialectal system where each reinforces the behaviour of the other. For example, a child unsure of being loved because he is perhaps jealous of a newborn baby may, as a last desperate attempt to get attention, do something aggressive towards it—and is at least 'rewarded' by a spank, which is better than being ignored!

Between the extremes of a healthy and normal reaction to an environmental pressure which strains the power of adaptation of an otherwise satisfactorily developed child, and the reaction which in itself is abnormal because a prior conflict situation has resulted in an impairment of the capacity to adapt, all degrees and gradations of maladjustment exist. The reactions, too, of individual children vary in terms of their previous history, their temperamental endowment, and of the types of pressures to which they are subjected. For example, insecure children brought up in a fairly rigid and strict discipline at home are likely, turning in upon themselves, to become nervous and excessively well behaved; those who live in a group which is very unstructured and permissive, tend rather to become aggressive and turbulent, noisy and destructive. But these reactions are by no means invariable; there are, for example, many cases of children whose fierce aggression is a reaction against a discipline which they resent as unbridled power directed against them; and some who, seeing indifference or danger in an over-permissive world, react with intensified anxiety, obsessional rituals and the like.

Much the same considerations apply to schools, classrooms and teachers as apply to homes and families. We may just note that there are not a few children whose behaviour difficulties or emotional disturbances only show themselves at home. Conversely, schools, even school systems, and individual teachers may be conducive to maladjustment—even 'teach' it, in the case of some children.[5] As we have seen earlier,[6] there are points of strain—transition from infant to junior school, from primary to secondary, situations of accumulating failure for example—in any school system. The teacher's style may be such as to provoke aggressive responses,[7] or may only reward very few children and constantly destroy the confidence of others by sarcasm, 'picking on' or poor marks in spite of effort. Some sensitive children cannot even bear hearing others being shouted at. Some very intelligent children become bored because the work in school contains insufficient challenge, and in consequence either withdraw or amuse themselves and others by clowning or manipulating the teacher.

Another profoundly important aspect of school life which is frequently overlooked as a cause (and expression) of maladjustment is any disturbance in relations with contemporaries. From the age of 6 or 7 onwards through to adolescence, the group of others of similar age dominates a pupil's life in highly complex ways. To be isolated or rejected, a figure of fun or contempt, is extremely difficult for a child to bear: the dull, the handicapped, the disfigured, the noticeably ill-dressed or dirty, the exceptionally intelligent, may all be cast out in various ways and react with behaviour, at home or in school, which intensifies the disturbance. The child from a good home in a poor neighbour-hood whose parents wish to keep him apart and maintain their high standards, for example, may find himself in a very difficult situation of conflict at school—regarded as a model by some teachers and rejected by compan-ions—and at home where he is isolated from companionship.

We may perhaps sum up by suggesting that a piece of behaviour should only be considered as abnormal if it tends to set up an enduring barrier between the child and the groups of adults and other children which constitute his world, and to indicate a far-reaching system of disturbance or potential disturbance in his relationships with others. A child can be said to be maladjusted when he is unable, to a noticeable and incapacitating extent, to enter freely at his level of general maturity into the life of his group and to meet the demands made on him in a way which the group itself finds acceptable. Some children are aggressive and destructive in their relations with their peers; they may be indifferent to punishment and to adults generally. Others seem to be making adjustments which do not attract attention to themselves. They become notice-ably shy and withdrawn; always, at best, on the margins. In many of both general kinds, there is disturbance in school progress which may be a result or a contributory cause of the maladjustment.

But we should also stress that adjustment and maladjustment are relative terms which describe the results, as we see them, of a child's learning within a series of environments. The general trend of development towards the one or the other is the result of many interactions. The environment of home and of school provokes behaviour from a child; a child's behaviour provokes response from those around him; and either of these can be 'maladjusted'. And since maladjustment is learned in this way, it should be (at least theoretically) possible to modify or even fundamentally to change behaviour by changing the environmental response which it evokes and the pressures which cause it.

CRITERIA OF MALADJUSTMENT

Much current discussion of the signs of maladjustment and many theoretical postulates as to causes and cures are based upon studies carried out by those whose experience is confined to cases of clearly and seriously maladjusted children. Only too frequently such studies have been based on certain theoretical assumptions which tend to determine the data sought and the interpretations offered. Moreover, the social and cultural nature of any definition and therefore of any criteria of mental health and personal adjustment make comparisons from country to country, or even from one social group to another, somewhat precarious. Such studies as have been made on the basis of comparing abnormal groups with groups of normal children matched for such variables as socio-economic group, age, sex and level of intelligence, indicate that, whereas certain personal factors, signs of maladjustment and environmental influences are significantly more frequent in various types of maladjusted group, they are not absent from the lives of otherwise normal children.[8]

Furthermore, behaviour which at one age is normal may be a sign of maladjustment if it is persisted in when the child grows older. A good example of this is the temper tantrum, normal in the 2- to 3-year-old child but, at least in its primitive form, a serious sign of maladjustment in a 10-year-old. Even here, however, judgement is not simple. We lack really adequate knowledge of how far forms of behaviour at one age foreshadow adjustment or maladjustment at a later stage and in what circumstances. Although we have some measures of social competence[9] and social adjustment,[10] these tend to be tied to particular social and cultural circumstances, and to be phenomenological rather than based upon a systematic, theoretical framework derived from secure knowledge. Some groups accept behaviour from which, in other groups, the child is weaned; and within any one community—particularly, for example, in large towns—considerable variations in tolerance will be found from one social level to another.

In the lives of most children who subsequently develop satisfactorily there occur periods of considerable disturbance which, however, pass without more direct psychological assistance than a tolerant family or school can give, and also, it seems, simply as the result of maturation.[11] In one of the rare studies of the development of normal children, Cummings found in an unselected group of 239 children aged between 2 and 7 years in three infant-nursery schools in Leicester (United Kingdom) that, on average, each child showed between two and three 'emotional symptoms'[12] and that none was entirely symptom-free. She found also that certain symptoms (for example frequency of micturition, specific fears) were less common in older children, whereas others, notably day-dreaming and lack of concentration, were more so. Following up the same children six to eighteen months later, she found that there was a tendency for symptoms to fade with the lapse of time. But this was marked only with those children who at the time of the original study were in the younger group.[13] For example, after six months, 55·5 per cent of the children aged originally between 2 and 5 had improved as compared with 18·3 per cent of those aged originally 5 to 8; after eighteen months the proportions were respectively 86·6 per cent and 53·2 per cent. This seems to indicate that certain 'emotional symptoms' are normal to young children under 5 but tend to be signs of a persisting disturbance if they occur in older children. A number of children in her group were manifestly sufficiently disturbed to warrant further investigation and probably psychological help. Such children would be conventionally regarded as maladjusted; it is interesting to note that rather less than half improved more or less spontaneously in the eighteen-months period, while the remainder, though frequently evolving a different behaviour or attitude pattern, continued to be markedly unadjusted to school.

The many longitudinal studies[14] which were begun, particularly between the wars in the United States and those begun in the 1940s and 1950s, have tended to indicate two very important findings. Some forms of apparently maladjusted behaviour in young children disappear during childhood but reappear later, particularly in adolescence.[15] This would indicate that, even if the behaviour itself is not immediately seen as particularly serious, constructive, preventive action by parents aided by skilled counselling or by the school itself might well reduce disturbances which occur when the child is older and the chances of helping him are limited. The second series of findings is much more general and far-reaching. If we consider the whole range of factors—social disorganization, family tensions, illegitimacy, maternal deprivation, mild or even major physical handicap, and the like—we can see that, while any one singly or almost any combination may be associated with later maladjustment, this is not inevitably so; on the other hand, some children develop maladjustments where there are few if any apparently unfavourable circumstances.

This suggests an approach to the prevention of maladjustment which is very similar to that proposed for ensuring that a physical disability does not become a general personal and educational handicap—that is, the very early identification of children who are at risk and particularly of those in whose early lives there is more than one prejudicial circumstance.[16] Complementary to such a proceeding, which involves a considerable diagnostic sensitivity in the social and medical services concerned with very young children, provision is necessary to be sure that crises which arise in family or other circumstances affecting children (death of a parent, sudden major economic difficulty, hospitalization and the like) are rapidly known to a service[17] which can give support to child, family and school.

THE PREVALENCE OF MALADJUSTMENT

The difficulty of defining accurately what constitutes maladjustment, what is a sign of a transitory disequilibrium and what is sufficiently indicative of a serious disturbance to warrant intervention, special remedial action or removal to a special school or class, makes the estimation of the prevalence of maladjustment hazardous. Such evidence as there is, however, tends to indicate that both serious maladjustment and states of developmental difficulty are more common in children than is usually supposed. In estimating the need for provision of special classes and schools for maladjusted pupils, the Department of Education and Science in the United Kingdom gives[18] the figure of about 1 per cent of the population of school age. This, however, can be considered a conservative estimate made in terms of minimum administrative provision for special educational arrangements. There remains a much larger group of children who need some help themselves or whose teachers or parents may need advice. The numbers of these are difficult to estimate. In Table 2 are grouped the results of ten investigations covering the years 1920 to 1971, made in France, New Zealand, the United Kingdom and the United States. Perhaps the most striking point to emerge from this table is that, if we take the figures for the 'seriously disturbed', there seems to have been no significant increase in the last fifty years, although there are fluctuations from investigation to investigation. The range is from around 4 to 14 per cent, with a tendency to cluster at 6–7 per cent. On the other hand, the proportion showing some signs of disturbance seems to be of the order of 30–35 per cent.

In general, such estimates have been made to exclude those children whose sole symptom is educational retardation. It is found, however, that while some maladjusted children give very little sign in school of their difficulties, in others educational retardation is itself one, if not the only, obvious sign of maladjustment; conversely, many children who become retarded in school develop difficulties of personality or of behaviour as a consequence of their lack of success. Moreover, maladjustment, though it may differ in its forms of expression, is if anything more prevalent among handicapped, dull and intellectually retarded children than it is among those of normal or superior endowment. Hence, between the various groups somewhat artificially separated in this book, there is probably considerable overlap; and the figures given should be considered also in relation to the proportions of scholastic failure in primary and secondary schools.[19]

Statistics like this show the magnitude of the problem generally. Some of the real problems for teachers which they conceal are revealed by the details of four recent and very carefully conducted investigations (three British and one French).

CLINICALLY SIGNIFICANT CONDITIONS

The first investigation, referred to earlier in this book,[26] is that of Rutter, Tizard and Whitmore, who studied the prevalence of handicap in the total school population aged between 9 and 12 in the Isle of Wight. These workers applied a very severe criterion—that of 'clinically significant psychiatric conditions'—and found that 6·8 per cent of their sample could be described as seriously maladjusted. Applying equally severe criteria, the authors also

TABLE 2. Comparative table of estimated incidence of maladjustment: ten investigations[20]

Investigator	Source of information	Date	Sample size	Age range	Showing some symptoms of maladjustment (%)*	Serious maladjustment (%)	Total (%)
Burt (U.K.)	Case study	1920 approx.	391	7–13	31.4[21]	4	35.4
Wickman (U.S.A.)	Teachers	1927	870	6–12	42.0	7	49.0
McFie (U.K.)	Teachers	1934	697	12–14	*46.0*		46.0
Milner (U.K.)	Teachers	1935	1,201[22]	10–16	*17.0*		17.0
Rogers (U.S.A.)	Various 'indices' including teacher's ratings	1940	1,524	6–12 approx.	30.0	12.0	42.0
New Zealand (N.Z.) Ed. Institute	Teachers checked by psychologists[23]	1948–9	2,363	5–14	*7.6*		7.6
Heuyer (France) et al.	Teachers	1944	95,237	6–13	*28.6[24]*		28.6
Ulmann (U.S.A.)	Teachers	1950	810	14	22.0	8.0	30.0
Rutter (U.K.) et al.	Detailed study	1964	—[25]	9–12	*6.8*		6.8
Davie (U.K.) et al.	Teachers (structured guide)	1965	1,600	7	22.0	14.0	26.0

* The figures in italics are not differentiated between 'some' and 'serious'.

studied the prevalence of severe reading backwardness (a discrepancy between reading age and chronological age of *at least* twenty-eight months) and mental subnormality. Eight per cent of those with reading difficulties and 24 per cent of the intellectually retarded had marked emotional and behaviour disorders.

QUALITATIVE DIFFERENCES IN PROBLEM CHILDREN

The second study, by Davie, Butler and Goldstein,[27] carries us further into the detail, not so much of the very severely disturbed but of the prevalence and qualitative differences in various disturbances of behaviour, relations and feeling among 7-year-old children. The teachers of those children assessed their adjustment and behaviour in school at the age of 7 by means of the Bristol Social Adjustment Guide,[28] an instrument which asks teachers to identify particular forms of behaviour rather than to assess adjustment. It yields a score which places children in three groups: 'stable', 'unsettled' and 'maladjusted'. This categorization gives a distribution for the 7-year-olds of this sample of 64 per cent 'stable', 22 per cent 'unsettled', 14 per cent 'maladjusted'. The last figure is somewhat higher than those from other investigations listed in Table 2. It is conceivable that some of the apparently higher prevalence figures for maladjustment are due to the borderline separating 'unsettled' and 'maladjusted'—since together they give much the same order of prevalence as is found in other studies—and some of it may be due to the actual age of the children, who are just emerging from their infant schools.

SOCIO-ECONOMIC[29] AND SEX DIFFERENCES IN PREVALENCE AND TYPE

Of more interest is the relation between the proportions by socio-economic group. There is an increase of about 17 per cent in the prevalence of maladjustment as we go from social class I to social class V; but whereas in the non-manual groups of social classes I to III the incidence is between 6 and 9 per cent, there is a big jump between social class III non-manual (minor clerical and service employees) and social class III manual (skilled workers)—a difference of 5–6 per cent. The rise in prevalence from social class III manual to social class IV (semi-skilled workers) is also fairly marked, and there is a big rise between social class IV and social class V (unskilled labourers, etc.), where the prevalence is well over 20 per cent.

The picture which we get is of a relatively homogeneous, more or less middle-class group (social classes I to III non-manual) which is on the whole well adjusted—certainly to school; of a skilled and semi-skilled manual group (social groups III manual and IV), where about one child in six is presenting difficulties in his behaviour and social relations in school; and of an unskilled labouring group (social class V) where between one child in four and one child in five has marked problems of adjustment to school.

Some of this difference is undoubtedly due to the expectations of the schools themselves, being basically middle class, and to the emphasis in the behavioural guide used on social behaviour. But this is not true of the whole of the items: much of the behaviour reported would be judged abnormal by any standard and, as we shall see later, when the mothers are the reporters, they report difficulties which do not involve social interaction.

There are, too, marked differences between boys and girls both quantitatively and qualitatively. Rather more boys than girls were rated as maladjusted. Boys more frequently showed aggressive behaviour, tended to be more restless, having more 'difficulty in settling to anything for more than a few minutes'; girls, on the other hand, were more prone to thumb-sucking, nail-biting, and to be miserable and tearful. Nearly three times as many boys as girls showed 'anxiety for acceptance by other children', whereas more girls than boys were 'anxious for adult acceptance'—a trait particularly marked among working-class girls.

'WRITING OFF' ADULTS AND INCONSEQUENTIAL BEHAVIOUR

Perhaps the most striking finding is the number of children at this early age of 7 whose behaviour indicates that they have 'written off' adults—7 per cent of working-class boys and 3 per cent of working-class girls. Coupled with this to some extent is 'inconsequential behaviour'—that is, children who seem to have little or no regard for the consequences of their behaviour and who show frequent and recurrent misbehaviour. Here the sex differences are marked, girls showing this kind of behaviour less than boys; and so are the social-class variations: for every middle-class girl in this category (1 per cent of all middle-class girls), there are four working-class girls, six middle-class boys and ten working-class boys (10 per cent of working-class boys).

CULTURAL DIFFERENCES IN THE ACCEPTABILITY OF BEHAVIOUR

In this study, the mothers were also asked to report on various items of behaviour in their children as they saw them at home. In some respects the findings are similar to what is reported from the schools, but in others they differ importantly. Apart from thumb-sucking—which is more frequent in social class I than it is in social class V—wherever there are differences, behavioural difficulties are more frequently found in working-class groups. However, the inter-class differences are much less regular and there is no indication of the big jump between the non-manual social class III and the manual group. There are some indications that certain forms of behaviour—overt aggressiveness, temper tantrums, destructiveness of others' belongings for example—may be more accepted in some groups than in others, whereas the schools are much more normative in their expectations of behaviour. We might put it in another way and say that destructiveness seen in school in a child coming from a professional home may well be an indication of emotional problems. The same behaviour in a child from an unskilled working-class home—where it is five times as common—may only indicate that this type of behaviour is more accepted at home.

CULTURE CLASH[30]

When we look at figures like these we have to remind ourselves that not all of those included—even in the category of severe maladjustment—will be perceived by their teachers as presenting a problem in the classroom. Some children, for example, who are excessively compliant or unforthcoming, may be overlooked or even regarded as good pupils, at least until their capacity as revealed by their work is considered. By the same token, some children may well find themselves at odds with their school, not because they have any deep-seated emotional or behavioural problem, but simply because the forms of behaviour which they display, normal enough in themselves and in their own out-of-school background, do not accord with the general expectations of the teacher and the other children—and may, indeed, be difficult to tolerate.

This latter is particularly likely to be true of children who come from a markedly different culture, whether it is indigenous or that of an immigrant group. The problem which then faces the school, and any service concerned with children who present problems, is whether to help the child adjust to school—and so perhaps make difficulties for him in his out-of-school life—or encourage the teacher to tolerate different behavioural norms within the same school or class; a very difficult thing to do in practice, particularly if the behaviour concerned is aggressive, destructive, or very disturbing to the general life of the class.

FAILURE TO LEARN—DOES IT CREATE MALADJUSTMENT?[31]

Teachers are also concerned with children who, for a variety of reasons, fail to profit fully from their schooling. It should be said, at the outset, that failure to learn tends to mean different things and to be more or less serious according to the expectations which adults and other children set up, as well as being a function of the inherent importance of what is to be learned. In school systems which set a heavy premium on particular forms of intellectual success, which stress inter-individual competition and the like, failure in particular aspects of school work can be very destructive for individuals whose development is otherwise healthy and balanced.

The question which we must ask is whether failure in school creates maladjustment or whether maladjustment is the root cause of failure. Simply to put the question in this way reveals that such a dichotomy does not accord with what we know about children and their learning. Children's ability to learn varies for both genetic and environmental reasons, and at different stages of development different kinds of learning become possible. The difficulty with which the schools have to contend is that (perhaps within wider limits of tolerance than are usually applied) they have an essentially normative function, that there are 'growth tasks' set by some conception of what is normal for children to be and to learn and, quite apart from what any particular teacher may expect, there are expectations within out-of-school groups (normally, of course, the family), failure to meet which may become a focus of anxiety. This, it should be remarked, is true whether we consider such things as reading or writing, or more obviously social forms of behaviour such as the ability to inhibit impulse or restrain anger in frustration. In this sense any marked discrepancy between what the child can do, any failure to conform to reasonable expectations—and 'reasonable' must here mean based upon experience of the average capacity of individuals to conform—is maladjusted or unadjusted. One notices at once the essentially cultural and valuative loading of such a postulate, as well as the fact that the demands to adjust may be set so high that none or few are able to conform, or so low that all or most can.

What we find in practice—if we take learning to read as an example—is that the majority of children can conform to the expectation that they will learn to read at the latest around the age of 7 or 8; but there will be some who do not. Among those who do not, there will again be some who, initially at all events, fail to do so simply because their ability to learn is markedly below average, and others who fail to do so for apparently non-cognitive reasons. Common experience also suggests that those who fail initially simply because of inadequate ability or inadequate prior learning may, if their initial lack of success has not been carefully handled, continue to fail, even though greater maturity makes success possible.

EMOTIONAL DISTURBANCE AND FAILURE TO LEARN

We can gain some estimates of the relation between emotional disturbance and cognitive failure—taking reading as the criterion—from the Isle of Wight study and the National Child Development Study (NCDS, 1958). The Isle of Wight project isolated a group of children whose reading age was twenty-eight months or more behind their chronological age—a serious degree of retardation in children between the ages of 9 and 12 (6·6 per cent of their whole sample). Of these, slightly more than half were twenty-eight months or more retarded compared to their general operational intelligence. Eight per cent of this group with a marked reading difficulty, not obviously related to low intelligence, had also marked emotional and behavioural disorders. On the other hand, of the intellectually retarded and backward readers, 24 per cent were markedly disturbed as well. Davie, Butler and Goldstein (NCDS, 1958) adopted a somewhat less stringent criterion of reading difficulty, taking the lowest 12 per cent of scores on a standardized group reading test. Using the 'maladjustment' score on the Bristol Social Adjustment Guide as a cut-off, these workers found that 37 per cent of their backward readers were also maladjusted and a further 35 per cent regarded as 'unsettled'. The comparable figures for children whose reading was progressing normally were 20 per cent unsettled and 10 per cent maladjusted. Of the virtual non-readers at age 7, 54 per cent were 'maladjusted'.

There is a considerable discrepancy between these two inquiries, which in part at least is due to the very different degrees of stringency in the criteria used and to the fact that one rests upon an individual *psychiatric* diagnosis, the other on teachers' observations of mainly social behaviour. There is, too, a difference in the age and circumstances of the two groups of children, the Isle of Wight group being older and in their junior schools, whereas the national sample is of 7-year-olds at the end of their infant school years. It is possible that behaviour is more varied at 7 than at a later period and, of course, much behaviour regarded by teachers as a sign of maladjustment—and which is, indeed, in the school context, both disturbed and disturbing—would not be taken as seriously by a psychiatrist concerned with the deeply abnormal.

But, with whatever caution we interpret these figures, the association between reading failure—and probably other forms of failure to learn—and emotional disturbance seems to be clear; equally one might suppose that the relation is in most cases reciprocal. From the teacher's point of view, this suggests that either behavioural or emotional disturbance is at any age a danger signal that learning failure may follow; similarly, failure to learn, for whatever reason, is a cue for action before it has emotional consequences of a lasting and compounding sort.

The possible reason for this, even when we are not considering the group of children who fail conspicuously but rather those who, according to their mothers, show some signs of disturbance at home—thumb-sucking, bed-wetting, nightmares, abdominal pain or recurrent vomiting—is indicated by our third example, which comes from another longitudinal study of a sample of children born in March 1946. Douglas[32] found that at 11, children with three or four such symptoms made on the average significantly lower scores on the group tests both of ability and attainment, and had tended to deteriorate in their general performance since the age of 8. Teachers too found that children with two or more such symptoms were poor workers, lacked concentration and had difficulties with their classmates.

PERSISTENCY OF CHARACTERISTICS

Later, at ages 13 and 15, the pupils in this same study were assessed by their teachers for their behaviour and for their attitude to work. In general, the assessments made of their attitudes to work remained the same at these two ages as they were in the primary school—the hard workers were still the hard workers. At the secondary stage the hard workers tended to be rated high for classroom behaviour by their teachers; higher in the selective, more academic, than in the non-selective schools. Douglas also found that the hard-working and well-behaved pupils, already drawing ahead in ability and attainment at 8, improved their position still more as compared to the troublesome poor workers at the secondary stage (a difference of 11·3 points, two-thirds of a σ on a standardized scale). The troublesome and poor workers left early, especially from the non-selective schools—94 per cent of the girls by the age of 15 plus.

This study also inquired of the teachers concerning behaviour and personal characteristics, such as nervousness, attention-seeking, competitiveness, aggressiveness, ability to make friends, energy, anxiety, and attitudes towards criticism and punishment, while the pupils themselves completed a self-rating inventory, which gave scores on 'neuroticism' and 'introversion–extraversion'.

Whereas the troublesome pupils were not only on the average poorer in performance than the rest and had deteriorated over the five or so years of their primary and secondary education, those among them rated as highly nervous or highly aggressive, though scoring on average below the others, did not get relatively worse during their school careers. However, there is a clear distinction all through between those rated nervous and those rated aggressive: the former were considered by their teachers to be hard-working although their success in school was moderate; the latter were likely to be considered troublesome in school, more frequently playing truant and neglecting their work.

When the teachers' ratings and the self-ratings of the pupils are combined, the picture emerges very clearly. The group which had high ratings for nervousness and/or aggressiveness, and a number of symptoms and high neuroticism scores, differed on the average from those who were low on these, by some 8 points of standardized score at age 15—and this discrepancy had consistently increased since the age of 8.

AN INTENSIVE FRENCH STUDY

A study by Chiland,[33] which is the fourth of our examples, is very different in style and in execution from those hitherto discussed, but confirms and illustrates from a very different group the findings of the others. She took as subjects all children entering a particular primary school at the age of 6 in a *quartier* of Paris: sixty-six children in all—a sample, she shows, which is reasonably representative of urban primary school children in France. These children and their families were intensively studied throughout their primary school careers.

Chiland's study of the family backgrounds leads her to say that there are few indeed without some psychological or other condition which might constitute a handicap in the growth of its children. However, she distinguishes three groups: those substantially without psychological difficulty (about a quarter of all families); those with a constellation of difficulties not of a markedly serious kind (about half); and those where clearly psychopathological difficulties were present (about a quarter). There is a clear social difference in incidence, a greater number of problem families being found in the lower social groups. There seem to be two broad causes for this which overlap; parents themselves having had difficulty in school because of psychological disturbance; and psychological difficulties arising from or aggravated by living conditions associated with socio-economic difficulties.

SCHOOL SUCCESS AND ADJUSTMENT OF CHILDREN FROM PROBLEM FAMILIES

In the first of Chiland's three groups, the children's I.Q.s ranged from 99 to 135 and their initial level was either maintained or increased during the period of the study. Their attainments in school were normal or accelerated. In the second group, the range of I.Q. was from 74 to 129. In the course of their schooling, ten out of the thirty-four children concerned showed a marked fall in I.Q. (more than 7 points). Only nine of the children were in classes normal for their age or better; all the rest were retarded, eight seriously so. Not all the children who were retarded were maladjusted, but by any criterion many were. In the third group, which was really two sub-groups—the one with serious parental disturbance but without aggravating social difficulties, the other in both socially and psychologically unfavourable circumstances—the picture was much more serious. In spite of the marked difficulties of one or both parents, two of the fifteen children seemed to be stable (both from the first sub-group) and two others better than could be expected; all the rest had great difficulties. In the first sub-group (I.Q. range 85–130), four showed a decline in I.Q. and six out of the eight were backward in school. Of the seven in the second sub-group (I.Q. range 78–100) one only showed a fall in I.Q., though all had a massive retardation in school.

TESTED INTELLIGENCE AND EMOTIONAL DISTURBANCE: CHANGES IN I.Q.

As a result of these and other observations on the growth of the children, Chiland underlines two conclusions. The relation between tested intelligence at, say, 6 years and the child's true ability is a complex one in which genetic and environmental factors enter in very different ways according to circumstances. She suggests that a low level of measured ability is only too often a 'scarring over' of childhood sufferings; a form of stability acquired after phases of disequilibrium, a calming down of the torments of the affective life at the expense of intellectual investment and growth. Secondly, she points out that the correlation between the child's attainment in his first school year and his subsequent educational development is closer than that between his measured ability at 6 and his subsequent attainment. In initial adjustment to school, the quality of the home environment seems to be determinant and continues to affect deeply how he continues to progress over the whole of his schooling. Finally, putting these observations together, she draws attention to the immense importance clinically of changes in I.Q. in the course of the primary years.

THE STABILITY OF PATTERNS OF LEARNING AND BEHAVIOUR

From all of these longitudinal studies, a number of striking tendencies emerge. The first and most evident one is that at least by the age of 7 or 8, and probably much earlier, patterns of learning and behaviour and general features of personality have emerged which in the usual circumstances of home and school are relatively stable throughout school life and which, if they are maladjusted, lead to poorer than average levels of attainment, early school leaving, and, in a proportion of cases though by no means in all, to delinquencies of varying degrees of seriousness. There are, too, quite marked social and sex differences. Girls throughout seem to be more stable and better motivated than boys, less likely to be aggressive, more likely to be nervous and neurotic, less likely to be delinquent.

GREATER DIFFICULTIES FOR WORKING-CLASS CHILDREN

We gain too from the study of 7-year-olds, a picture of the greater difficulty for working-class children, particularly those from the homes of unskilled workers, to adjust to the expectations of their schools and teachers, and to some considerable extent an indication that family norms and school norms may be in conflict.

It is also quite clear that poor educational performance is always a sign to be taken seriously, even at 7. However, the Isle of Wight investigation, in common with other work, shows that this is by no means always done and many children are left to flounder. Of the very severe cases of educational backwardness in the Isle of Wight, 'most received no special help in reading'. Even of the 7 per cent of children with what were considered clinically significant psychiatric conditions, only one in five was receiving treatment and in nine cases out of ten the difficulties had not been expertly diagnosed.

MALADJUSTMENT AND ALIENATION FROM SCHOOL

Perhaps the most serious fact to emerge is the number of children, particularly boys and particularly those in the least-favoured socio-economic groups, who appear to have written off adults as early as the age of 7 or who are markedly unforthcoming. When we link this with the findings concerning the relation between early leaving, particularly from non-selective but also from selective schools, and poor work attitudes, difficult behaviour or signs of personality disturbance, we begin to glimpse something of a pattern of alienation beginning very early in childhood and persisting as an accumulating indifference or hostility coupled with intellectual (and not merely formal educational) under-functioning.

A good many of such children, as well as others, also fall into a group displaying 'inconsequential behaviour', which is particularly characteristic of working-class boys and comparatively rare among middle-class girls. Such children, because they seem to have no regard for consequences or even fail to foresee them, can be highly disruptive in class, even at the age of 7. Later, some at least of these children become the uncontrollable and often violent adolescents whom no treatment or punishment appears to touch.

All the studies of educational failure, maladjustment, delinquency and the like unite in pointing out the relation between aberration of behaviour or development and a constellation of features in the home background—divorce, separation, illegitimacy, family strife and tension, absence of fathers, prolonged chronic illness, psychiatric disturbance—and with what might be called socio-demographic conditions—large families, overcrowding, urban slums and so on. However, although the associations are strong, they do not appear in themselves to be directly causal. On the whole, while adverse features occur much more frequently in the backgrounds of failing children than they do with normally developing ones, some—even a majority of—children succeed in spite of a number of adverse circumstances; and some children fail even when the circumstances seem favourable. The likelihood of failure—in learning, in general emotional and personality development—does, however, increase roughly proportionately to the number of adverse factors in the individual's life; moreover, the factors seem in some ways to be associated—for example Douglas[34] found that children with high aggression ratings had also had a large number of accidents in the first eleven years of their lives. It will be remembered too that only two children out of fifteen from the highly abnormal families in Chiland's inquiry progressed apparently normally.

It also seems to be clear that the major origins of much problem behaviour lie outside the classroom and to this extent outside the teacher's control. The child-rearing styles of the parents, the amount of interest they display or are permitted, by their physical and economic circumstances, to display in their child's progress, their declared or unexpressed attitudes to school, and their own educational history all seem to be closely associated with the attitudes and behaviour of their children.

PREVENTION AND REMEDY

Much of the evidence seems depressingly deterministic. Chiland documents the cycle of deprivation and neurosis; disturbed families falling in the economic scale and producing failure and disturbance in their children. Douglas, who has followed his subjects into adolescence, shows how patterns of maladjusted response seem not to change but rather to intensify over the period of schooling. Yet, whatever the provocative circumstances of a child's early environment, it is clear that we are not dealing with simple cause and simple effect; we are dealing with behaviour which is learned. If this is so, then maladjustment is preventable and to some considerable extent should also be curable. The small group of children pathologically abnormal from birth or soon after can certainly be helped (but perhaps not enabled to develop entirely satisfactorily) if they are recognized early enough and their parents assisted to adapt family upbringing to their special needs. So too children whose childhood is rendered abnormal by severely disturbing experiences and by their consequences—children who lose their mother in the first two or three years of life, or who have to spend long periods in hospital, for example—can, if measures are taken at once, be protected from the worst consequences of deprivation or shock. There is, additionally, the special problem of families where one or more parent is psychotic, or severely neurotic, and who may require continuous support.

But the majority of personality deviations, behaviour and habit disorders, and the like, arise from mistakes in parental upbringing, especially, but by no means exclusively, in the pre-school years; in many, too, living conditions directly or indirectly affect the parents' ability to cope. Social action to improve physical living conditions, and particularly to remove the necessity for mothers of children under 3 to work for long hours outside their homes (or to provide a high and stable level of care for their children if they do), will do something to make it easier for parents to bring children up adequately: but by themselves, however necessary and helpful, social and economic measures do not remove the causes of human inefficiency and inadequacy. If we wish to break the cycles of deprivation and of neurosis, we have to supplement physical improvements in the environment by practical and tactful education of parents so that, understanding the psychology of their children, they can, within the restrictions imposed by urban life and the contemporary shortage of living space, satisfy their needs in ways which are not merely minimally undamaging but genuinely constructive.

JUVENILE DELINQUENCY

Some maladjusted children become delinquent, and aggressive forms of maladjustment are particularly liable to make children and adolescents delinquency-prone. But, although most delinquency could be said to represent deviant behaviour, much of it is the expression of a clash of social norms, or a phenomenon of a particular reference group, or on a kind of limit-testing behaviour found as a likely accompaniment of adolescent development. A clash between a young person and the law is always serious, but particular delinquencies or categories of crime conceal a great complexity of human behaviour, a great variety of 'causes' and a correspondingly subtle set of considerations which we must bear in mind if we are to take preventive and constructive action to reduce delinquency rates.

PREVALENCE

Delinquencies committed by young people in the second decade of their lives form a significant proportion of all crime. About 50 per cent of all convictions for indictable offences in England[35] are for crimes by young persons between 10 and 21, proportionately more than double what would be expected from the proportion of the age group in the population. Convictions are most frequent between the ages of 12 and 20 with a peak in the mid-teens. It also seems, in general, in developed countries that—at least since 1958[36] and possibly steadily since the late 1930s with a dip in the immediate postwar years—there has been both an over-all increase in juvenile delinquencies and a tendency for there to be more offences of violence committed by the 17–20 age group. Most of those who are convicted (70 per cent or thereabouts) are first offenders who never appear again, and the proportion of those who commit more than two offences is low. Nevertheless, estimates made on the basis of figures in the 1960s suggest that the chances of a boy being convicted once for an indictable offence before he is 21 are between 12 per cent and 20 per cent.[37] If we include non-indictable offences—such as malicious damage, insulting behaviour and taking away motor cars—then the chances seem to be higher.

THEFT

However, by far the largest category of crime in general and particularly of juvenile delinquency is made up of theft of one kind or another, including breaking and entering. In the United Kingdom between 70 and 80 per cent[38] of all male crime and 90 per cent of delinquencies of boys of 14 and under, and 85 per cent of offences by those aged between 14 and 16 (breaking and entering being higher—33·1 per cent—in this group), is of this kind. A French study[39] gives a somewhat different picture: thefts of vehicles of all kinds 42 per cent; thefts from cars, shops, etc., 21 per cent; and thefts of money with or without breaking and entering, 16 per cent. Violence and robbery constitute a much smaller proportion of adolescent crime: 8·6 per cent of all delinquencies in the French figures for 1968; and, in the English ones, rising from 1·5 per cent of all offences committed by boys under 14 to 11·9 per cent of those of males in the age group 17–21. The figure for males of all ages is 8 per cent. So far as girls are concerned, at all ages the incidence is between one-tenth and one-sixth that of boys.

VIOLENCE

What then we are speaking of when we talk of juvenile delinquency, in the developed countries at all events, is mainly a male phenomenon of theft of various kinds, with violence coming a long way behind, and being characteristic much more (11·9 per cent) of late adolescent boys. Much of the theft (67·2 per cent of the cases in the French study) is the work of gangs of boys or young men rather than of isolated individuals. A study of delinquent violence[40] made a considerable time ago suggests, too, that only 6 per cent of incidents led to serious injury or death, and that for the rest, there were three roughly equal groups: youngsters brawling among themselves; fights with the police in resisting arrest; and attacks made in the course of thefts. In most cases the actual injury was relatively trivial or technical. However, a small minority of late adolescents are as dangerous as anyone can be and, as a crime, robbery with violence is most frequent in the age group 17–21. About half the murders committed in the course of robbery or other similar crimes are committed by young men, some as young as 16 or 17.[41] More recently, there seems to have been an increase in violence and violent vandalism associated with football matches and other sporting events, and with political demonstrations of various kinds.

Delinquency statistics comprise only those cases that come before the courts or, at the best, those known to the police. They will vary from time to time in any one country and between countries according to the ways in which they are recorded, according to changes in the law, and according to the vigilance and policy of the police at the time. For example, between 1955 and 1962 convictions for drinking offences by juveniles from 14 to 16 more than trebled in the United Kingdom, largely due to the number of reported transgressions of the law by under-age adolescents trying to be served in public houses. Similarly, a drive against soliciting in the streets led to a marked rise in convictions for sexual offences. On the other hand, certain types of theft—pilfering from shops and motor vehicles, for example—have shown a real increase closely correlated with other changes like the number of motor vehicles registered.[42]

UNRECORDED DELINQUENCIES

Studies of 'unrecorded delinquencies' in many parts of the world[43] provide an important gloss on the official records. They suggest that the incidence of minor delinquencies at least is much greater and more widespread among adolescents than official records imply, although more serious offences seem to be less frequent in non-convicted groups. The socio-economic differences in prevalence are less marked than studies of convicted delinquents suggest. Perhaps the most revealing aspect of these studies is that many of the acts committed, whether detected or not, are acts of social defiance, the result of group pressures, of sheer youthful exuberance, or a combination of them all. They also draw attention to something else: that recidivist offenders admit to around ten times as many violations of the law as do one-time offenders and, in the range of more serious offences, detected or otherwise, the difference between recidivists and others is even more extreme.

It seems likely that we are dealing with two rather different sets of phenomena. The first point to make is that conflict (for the most part undetected) with the law, social mores, rules and regulations is a normal part of growing up for very many young people, a part of the drive to assertion and independence, a testing of the limits; when the teens are over, by far the majority of young people become more willing and able to conform. Among the adolescent protesters is, however, a proportion who find the processes of teenage socialization markedly more difficult than do the majority; and their protests against their lot, or their high spirits and turbulence, bring them more than once into open and detected conflict with the law. But there is another, and much smaller, group of youngsters who will be seriously anti-social, violent and criminal for most of their lives, and who are likely to repeat their offences.

CAUSES

It is the existence of such very different groups and individuals that makes causal explanations (and consequential preventive and remedial measures) difficult. One cannot, for example, simply label as 'deviant' conduct in which half or more of an age group at times indulges, particularly if the behaviour itself represents conformity to a crowd, group or gang, membership of which is a common adolescent phenomenon and probably necessary as a transitional stage in socialization. On the other hand, studies of delinquents, and particularly of recidivists and serious offenders, tend to reveal constellations of factors in their early history, social circumstances, educational level and personality which are seriously adverse. Bowlby's[44] study of forty-four juvenile thieves, for example, revealed a close connection between an affectionless character, severe deprivation of maternal care and crime. Many other studies from Burt[45] onwards have drawn attention to a marked relation between delinquency and general failure in school (not necessarily due to lower than average intelligence); difficulties, abnormalities and lack of cohesiveness in the family life, particularly in relation to discipline;[46] the role of the father and maternal affection and supervision; and to an association of high delinquency rates with the poorer areas of large cities—in fact to just those constellations of difficulty and disturbance in development which lie behind much maladjustment, school failure and adult inadequacy.

Sociologists, from Durkheim onwards,[47] have been careful to point out that crime is normal and that the society's reactions—social solidarity against it, hostility and public labelling—are means of confirming a community's moral boundaries by constantly redefining and reaffirming what is permissible. Many acts are at one time regarded as criminal and at another simply as innovative protest or mere eccentricity. They would argue that delinquency and crime, being defined by what society says it is, can only reflect the attitudes of society.[48] Though perhaps not denying that some delinquents and criminals are deviant in a sense which could in almost any society be regarded as bad, basically they contend that norm-breaking behaviour is determined by the norms themselves.[49] Some go further to suggest that young offenders are on the whole normal members of a sick society, having learned, by seeing powerful and successful adults breaking the law, that the common goals of affluence, status and happiness are best attained that way.[50] They use the notion of 'anomie' (deriving from cultural chaos due to an imbalance between approved social goals and the means of attaining them open to the individual) and suggest that disadvantaged groups are tempted to take short cuts (delinquency) or to opt out by rejecting the goals and the means.[51]

If we put the sociological perspectives and the psycho-social ones together, they begin to make some sense of adolescent delinquency. Much of it is clearly traceable to the general intensification of emotional drives and instability, and especially the upsurge of aggression and independence characteristic of the adolescent period. It arises in part because adolescence coincides for many with such changes as leaving school and beginning work and because, whereas the misdemeanours of the child are likely to be infringements of the rules of the school or home, those of the adolescent and young adult bring them up against the laws of society. But there seem to be increasing numbers of children and of adolescents who break the law because they are conforming to the rules of a group or gang which, articulately or not, is at odds with the school or with society. Many such groups or gangs tend to exist in what some have called delinquent subcultures, and their existence is associated with depressed urban areas, with immigrant and/or coloured groups who are underprivileged, with high rates of poverty, adult crime and general social disaggregation. Some such groups, which include high proportions of the seriously disadvantaged through education, economics or colour, become seriously criminal and violent; others indulge in illegal acts as much for kicks and acting out a role to assert their manhood, or, in part at least, as a primitive form of protest against their lot. Other groups, without being criminal in the ordinary sense, make a more articulated form of protest. They embody a rejection of some aspects of the affluent, consumer-oriented society and the substitution for it of an idealistic and more or less legitimate form of adolescent culture. At times, this brings them into collision with the law by behaviour which they themselves do not regard as anti-social, immoral or even rightfully illegal—as for example certain forms of drug-taking,[52] or of social and political protest.

Among the membership of such groups, there will be many, even a large majority, of young people who are not in any true sense deviant or maladjusted, still less psychopathic; and a majority will have but one or no brushes with the law. But there will also be some who display—and often have displayed since childhood—patterns of behaviour and feeling which do portend continuing criminality. It will be recalled that a considerable proportion of boys in the NCDS (1958) longitudinal study had 'written off adults' as early as age 7. In the Douglas (1946) study, delinquency was associated with a record of markedly bad behaviour in school, truancy and a tendency to be perceived by teachers as aggressive. French[53] and American studies emphasize the importance of running away and truancy in childhood as premonitory signs; as is a history of court appearances before adolescence—the earlier in life the detected delinquency, the more likely is delinquency to persist. For the rest it seems clear that neglect or cruelty on the part of the parents, the absence of a parent, inconsistent or extreme discipline, a parent who is himself criminal, and a parental failure to teach adequate standards of behaviour, are all circumstances from which delinquency is likely to result. To these we can add the effect of delinquent neighbourhoods, and the continuing frustration and poor self-image built up in a child by continuing failure at school, not only in academic work itself but in the structure of relations with adults and with other pupils. Indeed, there is evidence which suggests that, at least in the case of pupils whose delinquency is not the result of very deep-rooted and long-standing personality difficulties, and even where the neighbourhood itself is one of high criminality and delinquency, school climates and organization can have a marked positive or negative effect on delinquency rates. In an area of East London, where about one boy in four on the average was likely to be convicted before reaching the age of 17 and where, in certain districts, it was as high as one in two, the proportions of boys convicted between 11 and 14 in the populations of different secondary schools in the area varied from as little as 0·9 per cent to as high as 19 per cent.[54]

PREVENTION AND REMEDY

Whether we are concerned with educational failure, with maladjustment in all its forms or with overt delinquency, prevention and remedy are not matters of symptomatic treatment or of simple measures of social action. The first and crucial area of action is the family, since it is in the family that the earliest education of the child takes place and, throughout the first two decades, the influences exerted by the family, either positively or by default, tend to prevail over those of the school or any other institution. But the family is set in an environment, in a socio-economic and broadly political framework which either hinders or facilitates its tasks—particularly at the extremes of economic deprivation or social disagregation. As the child grows older, and particularly in the course of the second decade, the influence of the group of contemporaries, the culture of the streets and the mass media become more influential especially in determining the forms which behaviour may take and the more manifest expression of underlying value systems.

Something can, and of course should, be done by direct action on those aspects of the physical and economic environment which make it difficult, if not impossible, to bring children up in satisfactory ways. But rises in standards of living, improved housing, the provision of better leisure facilities, health care and so on do not in themselves reduce the prevalence of educational failure, of maladjustment and of delinquency. Paradoxically, social and economic advance appears to be accompanied by rising delinquency rates, a greater proportion of social breakdown, divorce, and little if any diminution in the number of failing or maladjusted children in schools.

Broadly, and perhaps over-simplistically, we can allege two reasons for this. The first is that social and economic changes over the past six or seven decades have brought with them psychological tensions, stresses and possibilities which impose on individuals, children, adolescents and parents demands for adjustment greater than those of the more stable, more slowly changing societies of the past. 'Turbulence'[55] is a characteristic of our society and seems likely to increase. This makes the task of education infinitely more complex since it is not a matter of fitting a child to participate in a stable and predictable society but that of developing in each individual a capacity to withstand stress and uncertainty whilst making a succession of dynamic adjustments. Education has to be constructive and prospective rather than adaptive and conservative. Much maladjustment and delinquency can be viewed as due, in part at least, to a mismatch between the developed capacity of the individual to make continuing (but provisional and changing) adjustments and the constantly changing demands of his society—whether this is the child in his first contact with school, his father confronted with a change of job, an adolescent boy perceiving the contrast between visible affluence and his own deprived circumstances, or a girl confronted by her boy friend with a moral dilemma for which there are no clear and accepted rules.

The second reason why social, economic and other ameliorations of the environment do not by themselves bring about improvement is even more obvious. Like other administrative changes, they may remove hindrances, create opportunities and provide possibilities. By themselves, they do not cause those fundamental changes in human behaviour and attitudes on which depends any real alteration in the psychological factors contributing to maladjustment; nor do they remove or socialize the tensions and conflicts incidental to puberty and adolescence. Social and economic action must be accompanied by a directly constructive and educational use of the environment in which families and schools are involved together at all stages of growth.

THE SCHOOL

In childhood and adolescence the school, as the sole institution which touches all children and their families, has a big part to play both in the prevention of maladjustment and delinquency and in the cure of those whose development is awry. It is the task of the school to see that its demands for achievement and for adjustment are such as to be generally within the compass of its pupils' normal development, and to be ready to temper them considerably to individual variations in tolerance. Moreover, the teacher should recognize that some children take longer than others to adapt or may need a little friendly help at a critical moment. This is particularly true in the first school year, at periods of transition, and whenever an examination or other testing period is imminent.

There is, however, a limit beyond which a teacher in an ordinary class may not be able to tolerate maladjustments displayed, for example, in seriously aggressive behaviour or markedly bad work; moreover, those children whose maladjustment attracts little attention, the over-conscientious or very timid, may, though acceptable to the school as causing no trouble, need help beyond the power and the training of a teacher, preoccupied with thirty or forty children. Many such children can be helped by being put into a small group of eight or ten under a sympathetic and preferably specially trained teacher.[56] Such a group can be more tolerant and accepting of difficult behaviour, can give more creative and remedial outlets, and the teacher can build a closer, more personal contact with pupils and with parents. It has been shown that, with little if anything more than this, many children can be helped through a period of severe personality difficulties, until with increased age greater stability comes. In more serious cases and where the cause is clearly in the home, a period in such a class may support the child and prevent him from deteriorating whilst efforts are made to improve the family itself.

In some cases, the home circumstances are so bad and the pressures on the child so intense, that there is no alternative but, for a time at least, to send him to a residential school, or to place him in a hostel from which he can attend the ordinary school. The advantage of such a measure is that all the circumstances of the child's life can be controlled and the adults in his environment can adapt themselves to his needs whilst carrying out an intensive re-education.[57] This may be essential where the family is irretrievably pathological or for some reason cannot cope with the child or adolescent. The decision to remove a child from his home, though the temptation to do so is great when his troubles are clearly the result of parental mishandling, is not to be made lightly; moreover, it should be regarded essentially as a short-term solution for all but those few cases where it is totally impossible to help the child and his family mutually to adjust. This solution of a short-term stay, arranged usually with the consent of the parents, but sometimes by order of a juvenile or other court, is now provided in a number of European countries, including Austria, France, the Netherlands and the United Kingdom. In all these countries, however, emphasis is laid upon the exploration of alternatives such as temporary boarding out, hostel care, keeping the child and family together under supervision, and upon vigorous social work with the family so as to prepare for the child's return if he is removed for a period.

THE CARDINAL IMPORTANCE OF THE ENVIRONMENT

It is important, both in examining and in helping problem children, to emphasize the social and environmental aspects of their difficulties, since it is mainly through the educative or re-educative quality of the environment that remedy must come. It is true that many children, by the time they are referred to specialized psychological services, have so serious a disturbance, and one which has continued for so long, that they need very specialized and skilled individual help over a long period—special remedial education, behaviour modification or some other form of direct personal aid. But even in such cases, the treatment of the child alone is rarely sufficient. Most maladjustment or delinquency, as we have seen, is unlike physical disease, and is not a simple clinical entity referable to a direct single cause which, once removed, leaves all as before. The interacting factors which have modified, and continue indirectly to modify, the whole pattern of the child's learning have to be tackled. Hence, while in many cases a relatively small change in the environment may be all that is necessary or possible, the child himself cannot be helped in isolation; home and school are both directly involved, and from the outset should be called into collaboration.[58]

The weakness of much psychiatric and some psychological work in the past, its comparative inefficacy and the frequency with which, even if there is an immediate improvement, it is followed by a relapse, may be traced to the fact that psycho-therapy has been conceived on an old-fashioned model of disease and cure, and as such is inevitably ineffective.[59] This has indicated a 'treatment' of the individual aimed at restoring him to what he reputedly was. What we know of the genesis of most maladjustment suggests a prospective educational model concerned with positive change. It treats maladjustment as a learning problem both in its causes and in its remedies. The accent, therefore, is upon a close study and modification of the whole world of home and school in which the child lives and to which he has become maladjusted. It follows from such an environmental educational model that individual treatment, if it is used at all, is secondary to the involvement in a positive re-educational programme of all those who have to do with the child. While it may be necessary for the psychologist to take the lead in the examination of the child, in the planning of a programme to help and in the co-ordination of the measures taken, the success of any attempt will depend how far all those concerned—teachers, parents, doctors, psychologists, social workers—understand what is being done and why. In its turn, this directs our attention to the need, in any re-educational programme, of clearly defined goals understood and agreed to by all those concerned.

It will be noticed that what has been said is the reverse of the conventional wisdom which underlies many child guidance and delinquency clinics. It implies both a diagnosis and a treatment strategy which treats the child in all his social settings and tends more to an operant model of learning than to a pseudo-dynamic one; a social psychological rather than a psychiatric approach. The psychologist has a major role to play which is perhaps novel to those who have been trained only as psychometricians or clinicians, and see themselves as principally concerned with diagnosis and direct individual therapy. He should be able to understand the complex mechanisms of human social learning, and be present as a neutral observer in critical environments—like the classroom particularly, but the playground also and the home if possible. His task is to study the social system in which children develop and to tease out the ways in which the dysfunctional behaviour of any maladjusted child or adolescent may be being reinforced unconsciously, by the teacher, by the parent, by other children or indeed by an environment which only provides delinquent outlets for adolescent drives. Armed with this knowledge and without, of course, being destructively critical, he can then begin to sensitize his teaching colleagues and at least some parents to the effect of their responses on a child, and help them to change their own behaviour in positive ways. It is possible too, for a teacher who has generally good relations with his or her pupils to be helped by a psychologist to bring about an increased understanding in the children themselves of the 'whys' of behaviour, and to enlist their help with individual companions under stress. The psychologist, in fact, may not himself be directly in contact with the child. He will be attempting to help others reshape the environment to make it therapeutically educational.

Behaviour difficulties, habit disorders, scholastic failure, character or personality deviations and delinquencies of any kind, are always matters to be taken seriously—even though they may seem to be slight and, in many cases, prove transitory. All children from time to time, and especially in early childhood and in early adolescence, display signs of maladjustment and disturbance, which indicate strains in their lives; these are normal, even healthy, signs of growth. It is important that the teacher[60] and the parent should recognize these for what they are and should have the understanding to help the young to confront their difficulties and stresses. The problem is to distinguish those cases which merely demand such understanding and relatively short-term help, from those which have need of a more massive intervention or modification of the normal home or school environment. On the teacher, particularly, falls the duty of calling expert psychological help to his assistance, when a child's difficulties persist and there is reason to suppose that something more than tolerance or firmness from the school is necessary. This expert help should be freely available and on as informal a basis as possible. While no doubt such special services as child psychiatric clinics outside the ambit of education are at times necessary and valuable, there is no real substitute for a school psychological service[61] as fully integrated as possible with the classrooms, the teachers, the families and their children. Only in this way can developmental difficulties be dealt with as they arise, by consultation among those concerned without the cumbersome and often disturbing procedures of referral and labelling. What is perhaps even more important is that psychological interventions of the kind described, and concerned with the social psychology of groups, have an important effect upon the school and the teachers concerned, rendering them more able to deal themselves with problems as they arise. ✕

CONCLUSION

It is quite clear from what has been said that prevention and remedy are no simple matter. Indeed, with delinquency, as with maladjustment, the success rates of the various measures which have been taken and rigorously investigated are not high. Most of the work directly concerned with delinquents has attempted to assess the effectiveness of various forms of disposal after conviction—probation, intermediate treatment by attendance at special centres, assignment to more or less custodial treatment or educational institutions, and so on. It seems that the best prediction of whether offences will be repeated or not is not the form of treatment but the characteristics of the offender, of his offence and of his personal background[62]—that is to say, whether the delinquent act is an expression of a long-standing maladjustment, an ingrained adverse socialization or, more simply, the result of immediate growth stresses. One thing does seem to be clear—while some sort of punishment may be necessary to mark that an offence has been committed, incarceration seems to be useless either as a deterrent or as a cure.

We have less evidence, and none of a direct kind, that the various measures proposed by reformers as preventive of delinquency are effective; and by the nature of preventive and constructive work we might expect this to be so. However, much delinquent behaviour, as we have seen, is learned by otherwise 'normally' developing children; much is clearly the result of delinquent contexts; much is a by-product of legitimate protest against unsatisfactory aspects of an individual's life or broadly unsatisfactory aspects of society; only some of it represents serious and deep-seated problems in the personality of the individual. If this is, in fact, an adequate diagnosis, real prevention will only come by intervening positively in the education of all children in the ways which have been suggested earlier.[63] Particularly will this be seen as necessary for those from the more vulnerable groups. We shall equally, so far as adolescents are concerned, try to see that the natural and healthy protest, and the aggressive drives towards independence and testing the limits of society's tolerance, are accepted by adults and directed in positive and constructive ways, inside the micro-society of the school and outside. We shall recognize the importance of discussing with the young the anomalies, deprivations and other ills that afflict them personally and society as they see it, and of helping them to understand how these arise and how they may be changed.

This is not solely a matter for schools which cater for adolescents, which in any case come late in the developmental process. As with other handicapped groups, infant and primary schools must be concerned at the earliest moment with any individual or group which is clearly at risk of delinquency, maladjustment and failure. Children who are failing to settle in school, children who are inconsequential in their behaviour, who are markedly aggressive, who are under social or family stress, or who simply come from known delinquent neighbourhoods, must all be the target of special attempts to help. It must be reiterated that measures of any kind which are taken as the result of breakdown are nearly always less effective than those aimed to prevent it. Next to the home, the school has the most to do with the lives of children and adolescents; and education is dedicated to changing and improving individuals. Whatever else we may do, it is basically with the school that we must start, and it is from the school, as the centrally placed institution, that educational services to improve family life, to provide constructive leisure and to give remedial help where necessary can and should start, and be conducted without the labelling and stigma inherent in services normally only called upon when a breakdown has occurred.

NOTES

1. Precise estimates are difficult to obtain because of differences of opinion as to what constitutes an inherent anomaly of temperament or a clearly psychiatric illness in children. The experience of child guidance centres and clinics in the United Kingdom, however, tends to suggests that only some 10 to 15 per cent at most of *all cases referred* to such clinics fall into that group. If we take into account all forms of maladjustment—major and minor—the proportion is very much lower still. (See Burt, C. Symposium on psychologists and psychiatrists in the child guidance service, *Br. j. educ. psychol.* (Edinburgh), vol. XXIII, pt. 1, Feb. 1953). It will be remembered that in the study of Rutter, Tizard & Whitmore (op. cit., note 2, chapter 1) 6·8 per cent of children had 'clinically significant psychiatric conditions', many of whom seemed to have neurological damage.
2. See: Chazan, M. Maladjusted children. *In*: Mittler, P., ed. op. cit., note 2, chapter 3.
3. An elaborate triaxial scheme is proposed by participants in the third WHO Seminar on Psychiatric Disorders in Childhood (Rutter, M., et al. A triaxial classification of mental disorders in childhood. *J. Child psychol. & psychiatr.* (Elmsford, N.Y., Association of Child Psychology and Psychiatry; Oxford, England), vol. 10, no. 1, 1967) suggest that such disorders should be classified by: (*i*) clinical syndrome (normal variation, adaptation reaction, specific developmental disorder, conduct disorder, neurotic disorder, psychosis, personality disorder, psychosomatic disorder, etc.); (*ii*) intellectual level; and (*iii*) associated or aetiological factors. There are of course other classifications, for example that of D. H. Stott (*The social adjustment of children: manual of the Bristol Social-Adjustment Guides*. London, U.L.P., 1971), which tends to insist upon a genetic and perinatal element in causation; and that of Eysenck whose introversion-extraversion and neuroticism-stability axes are also considered to be powerfully determined by heredity and to have a biochemical or physiological basis (Eysenck, H. J.; Rackman, S. *The causes and cures of neurosis*. London, Routledge & Kegan Paul, 1965). Psychoanalytically oriented workers use other types of classification; as do the learning theorists. There is a fundamental difficulty in getting agreement to any classification (and in interpretation if we had one) because of theoretical cleavages on the one hand and the evaluative component in symptom or behaviour description on the other. A third problem is that there is in maladjustment a large social element, and in understanding behaviour and its causes we have also to understand the past history and immediate life-space of the individual.
4. We are here in the presence of particular problems of degree, involving philosophical, ethical and social conditions of great complexity. For example, some argue that the modern family

and/or the society which surrounds it is pathogenic, itself 'sick', and that reactions such as schizophrenia are normal but that the means taken to treat them maintain the social pathology. See: Laing, R. D. *Self and others*. New York, Pantheon Books, 1970.

5. See Power, M. J., et al. Delinquent schools. *New Soc.* (London), 19 October 1967.
6. See the first volume in this series, *Constructive education for children*, chapter 11, p. 251 ff. and p. 274 ff.
7. See the second volume in this series, *Constructive education for adolescents*, chapter 7, p. 247–51.
8. Classic examples of the study by means of control groups of the complex of associated personal and social factors in school maladjustment and in delinquency are the two studies by Burt (*The young delinquent*. London, U.L.P., 1925.; *The backward child*. note 26, chapter 2).
9. For example, The Vineland Social Maturity Scale (Doll, E. A. *Manual*. Minneapolis, Minn., Educational Test Bureau, Educational Publishers Inc., 1947; The Vineland Social Maturity Scale. *Train. sch. bull.* (Vineland, N.J., American Institute for Mental Studies), vol. 32, 1935; A preliminary standardization of the Vineland Social Maturity Scale. *Am. J. Orthopsychiatr.* (New York, American Orthopsychiatric Association, vol. 6, 1936); and the British Standardization (Lunzer, E. A. The Manchester scale of social adaptation. Slough, NFER, 1961).
10. The Bristol Social-Adjustment Guide.
11. See: Valentine, C. W. *The difficult child and the problem of discipline*. London, Methuen, 1940; Valentine, C. W. *Abnormalities in normal children*. Highbury, National Children's Home, 1951.
12. Cummings, J. D. The incidence of emotional symptoms in school children. *Br. J. educ. psychol.* (Edinburgh), vol. XIV, pt. 3, 1944. Cummings' list includes all those symptoms usually considered as possibly indicative of maladjustment and which can be observed in the classroom and playground. Those of most frequent occurrence were: excitability, restlessness (28·9 per cent); day-dreaming, lack of concentration, laziness (28·9 per cent); generalized anxiety, timidity and shyness (23·0 per cent); specific fears (22·2 per cent); lack of bladder control, frequency of micturition (21·3 per cent); nervous habits (18·9 per cent); cruelty, aggression (15·1 per cent); speech difficulties (14·2 per cent); lack of appetite, food faddiness (11·3 per cent); babyish behaviour, frequent crying (11·3 per cent); lying, stealing (10·1 per cent).
13. Cummings, J. D. A follow-up study of emotional symptoms in school children. *Br. j. educ. psych.* (Edinburgh), vol. XVI, pt. 3, 1946.
14. See Wall, W. D.; Williams, H. L. *Longitudinal studies and the social sciences*. London, Heinemann, 1970.
15. Kagan, J.; Moss, H. A. *Birth to maturity*. New York, Wiley, 1962; Bronson, W. C. Central orientations: a study of behaviour organization from birth to adolescence. *Child dev.* (Chicago, Society for Research in Child Development), vol. 37, 1966, p. 125–55.
16. For example, we know that illegitimacy, even in a relatively tolerant society, constitutes a handicap which suitable adoption may mitigate. In a study of a national sample of illegitimate children born in 1958 (National Child Development Study's 1958 cohort), Crellin, Pringle and West (*Born illegitimate: social and educational implications*. Slough, National Foundation for Educational Research in England and Wales, 1971) found that the illegitimate are at a potential disadvantage from the outset because of their mothers' age—five times as many young mothers as in the normal sample—and because if the mother keeps her child she tends to sink in the social scale, with the concomitant of poor housing, mother at work and lack of a male parent. About one-third of these illegitimate children were adopted. These developed much more favourably than the non-adopted but still somewhat less so than the average of the legitimate. In 1969 (United Kingdom) 67,000 live births were illegitimate, and 73,000 were premaritally conceived and legitimized by later marriage—a rate of 45 per 1,000 in maternal age groups 15–44, and 62 per 1,000 in the age group 20–26.
17. Morse, W. C. *Crisis intervention in school mental health and special classes for the disturbed*. Ann Arbor, Mich., University of Michigan, 1968.
18. The Minister of Education (United Kingdom, 14 December 1972) gave 0·07 per cent of children as the figure for those in special schools and a further 0·02 per cent on waiting lists.

Most of the thirty-eight countries replying to the Unesco questionnaire and recognizing maladjustment as a problem (not all do), consider their provision to be inadequate. The American response states that only 13 per cent of those needing special education because of emotional disturbance are in fact getting it, as compared with an average figure for *all* handicapped of 36 per cent. See: Unesco, op. cit., note 72, chapter 2. Glidewell, in an unpublished report cited by Chiland (1971), concludes that 30 per cent of elementary school children (United States) pose problems of adaptation, and 9 per cent of them problems serious enough to warrant skilled attention, but that only 2–3 per cent are in fact referred to special services.

19. See the first volume in this series, *Constructive education for children*, chapter 11, p. 266 ff.; and the second volume, *Constructive education for adolescents,* chapter 5, p. 166 ff.

20. Burt, C. *The backward child*. 2nd ed. London, University of London Press, 1946; Wickman, E. K. *Children's behaviour and teachers' attitudes*. New York, Commonwealth Fund, 1928; McFie, B. S. Behaviour and personality difficulties in school children. *Br. j. educ. psychol.* (Edinburgh), vol. IV, pt. 1, 1934; Milner, M. *The human problem in schools*. London, Methuen, 1938; Rogers, C. R. Mental health findings in three elementary schools. *Ed. research bull.* (Columbus, Ohio, Ohio State University, College of Education), no. 21, 1942; New Zealand Educational Institute. *Emotional maladjustment in New Zealand school children*. Auckland, 1950; Heuyer, C., et al. *Le niveau intellectuel des enfants d'âge scolaire*. Paris, Presses universitaires de France, 1950; Ullman, C. A. *Identification of maladjusted school children*. Washington, Government Printing Office, 1952 (Public health monograph, no. 7); Rutter, M; Tizard, J.; Whitmore, K. op. cit., note 2, chapter 1; Davie, R.; Butler, N.; Goldstein, H. op. cit., note 8, chapter 1.

Of the 656 London school children studied by S. Isaacs and others (*The Cambridge evacuation survey*. London, Methuen, 1941), 155 were referred to the Child Guidance Clinic (23·6 per cent), 13 per cent were in need of skilled help and, of these, 4 per cent were cases of considerable severity. It will be observed that this group is rather special, since they were children abruptly removed from their homes in wartime and at a period of considerable general stress.

21. In *The backward child* (see note 20) p. 542, Burt gives figures for his control group of normal (i.e. not backward) children. This figure is the result of grouping various temperamental and emotional conditions. Burt points out that excitability (included in this figure—frequency for normals 9·7 per cent) is partly a characteristic of the social group from which these children were drawn.

22. Girls only. The investigation was carried out in five schools having a population drawn mainly from economically superior groups and having a progressive educational outlook.

23. Teachers' comments were checked by a committee of psychologists and doubtful cases ruthlessly eliminated. Only the results for urban populations are given as more comparable with those in the rest of the table.

24. This includes 24·7 per cent of children with personality difficulties and 3·9 per cent with speech difficulties.

25. The total population of one typical local education authority—rural, suburban and urban—studied in a very detailed way and with highly rigorous criteria. Children with maladjustments *not warranting psychiatric intervention* were excluded.

26. Rutter, M.; Tizard, J.; Whitmore, K. op. cit., note 2, chapter 1.

27. Davie, R.; Butler, N.; Goldstein, H. op. cit., note 8, chapter 1.

28. See note 3 to this chapter.

29. The socio-economic groups referred to are those of the Registrar General's (United Kingdom) classification based upon the employment of the head of the family. Social groups I and II are professional and administrative. Social group III is subdivided into non-manual employment—clerical and secretarial, retail trade, lower administrative and so on—and a skilled manual group. Social group IV corresponds to the semi-skilled manual workers, and social group V to the unskilled and casual occupations. The groupings are used primarily for census purposes and only roughly correspond to such important variables (for our purpose) as parental education, value systems in the home, parental rearing styles, and enlightened

interest in the progress of their children. Nonetheless, there are pervasive correspondences between socio-economic group and a whole range of other social and personal indicators, particularly at the extremes of social groups IV and V—for example in the use made of social and medical services, in the prevalence of educational backwardness, in early/late school leaving and so on. See: *Constructive education for children* chapters 6, 8 and 9.

30. The question as to whether a school *should* adjust its values to those of the homes of its pupils is a far from simple one. It is discussed in *Constructive education for children*, chapter 10, especially p. 195 ff.
31. The whole question of school failure is dealt with in *Constructive education for children*, chapter 11, section B.
32. Douglas, J. W. B. *The home and the school*. London, MacGibbon & Kee, 1964; Douglas, J. W. B.; Ross, J. M.; Simpson, H. R. *All our future*. London, Peter Davies, 1968.
33. Chiland, C. *L'Enfant de six ans et son avenir*. Paris, Presses universitaires de France, 1971.
34. Douglas, J. W. B.; Ross, J. M.; Simpson, H. R. op. cit., note 32.
35. Indictable offences are, in theory, the more serious crimes. Thus in the United Kingdom figures, larceny, breaking and entering, fraud, violence against the person, and certain sexual offences are included. Offences like common assault, drunkenness, malicious damage, taking away motor vehicles without the owners' consent, reckless, dangerous or drunken driving, offences by prostitutes, exhibitionism and homosexual importuning are excluded. Other countries do not make this distinction and direct comparisons of statistics are difficult to establish.
36. See Soulé, N.; Delaporte, J. C. Délinquence juvenile. *In*: Mande, R., Masse, N.; Manciaux, M., eds. op. cit., note 8, chapter 1.
37. Prys Williams, G. *Patterns of teen-age delinquency*. London, Christian Economic and Social Research Foundation, 1962; Radzinowicz, L. *Ideology and crime*. London, Heinemann, 1966; both cited by West, D. J. *The young offender*. Harmondsworth, Penguin, 1967.
38. West, D. J. op. cit., note 37, gives the following percentage figures for breaking and entering and for larceny from official criminal statistics for England and Wales: males 14 and under—breaking and entering 32·9 per cent; larceny 57·1 per cent; 14–16 years—33·1 and 51·6 per cent; 17–20 years—25·8 and 51·3 per cent. In France in 1968 the figure was 71·6 per cent for boys in the whole age group. Soulé, M.; Delaporte, J. C. op. cit., note 36, p. 493.
39. Soulé, M., Delaporte, J. C. op. cit., note 36 quoting a study in the Bouches-du-Rhône.
40. By Charlotte Banks in 1952, cited by West, D. J. op. cit., note 37.
41. West, D. J. op. cit., note 37.
42. Wilkins, L. T. *Social deviance*. London, Tavistock, 1964, cited by West, D. J. op. cit., note 37.
43. West, D. J. op. cit., note 37, citing British, Swedish, Norwegian and American research.
44. Bowlby, J. *Forty-four juvenile thieves*. London, Ballière, Tindall & Cox, 1946.
45. Burt, C. op. cit., note 8, see above; Glueck, S.; Glueck, E. T. *Unravelling juvenile delinquency*. Cambridge, Mass., Harvard University Press, 1950; Heuyer, G. *La délinquence juvénile*. Paris, P.U.F., 1969.
46. Andry, R. G. *Delinquency and parental pathology*. London, Methuen, 1960. L. T. Wilkins (*Delinquent generations*. London, HMSO, 1961) points to the relation between the absence of fathers from 1939–45 and a higher incidence of delinquency among children born in 1934–39.
47. Durkheim, E. *The rules of sociological method*. Chicago, Free Press, 1950; Mead, G. H. The psychology of punitive justice. *In*: Reck, A. J., ed. *Selected writings of George H. Mead*. New York, Bobbs-Merrill, 1964.
48. Changing attitudes to homosexuality and abortion are cases in point.
49. Phillipson, M. *Sociological aspects of crime and delinquency*. London, Routledge & Kegan Paul, 1971.
50. Sutherland, E. H.; Cressey, D. R. *Principles of criminology*. Chicago, Lippincott, 1955. Cited by West, D. J. op. cit., note 37.
51. Merton, R. K. *Social theory and social structure*. New York, Free Press, 1957. Cited by West, D. J. op. cit., note 37.

52. Drug-taking is dealt with fully in *Constructive education for adolescents* (the second volume of this work), chapter 5, section H.

53. Soulé, M.; Delaporte, J. C. op. cit., note 36; Glueck, S., Glueck, E. T. op. cit., note 45.

54. Power, J. J., et al. Delinquent schools? *New soc.* (London), 19 October 1967.

55. See Eisenstadt, S. N. Cultural settings and adolescence and youth in Hill, J. P. and Monks, F. J., *Adolescence and youth in prospect.* Guildford, IPC Science & Technology Press. This whole thesis is dealt with very fully in chapters 2 and 5 of *Constructive education for children* (the first volume of the present work).

56. Such classes have now been established in many countries where disturbed children attend for periods of up to nine months or a year, and where they can be given special supervision and individual help, as have adjustment groups which receive maladjusted children for periods of time during the week. The Inner London Education Authority (United Kingdom) was one of the pioneers of this kind of very valuable provision. This is described and the success evaluated in: Inner London Education Authority. *Survey into progress of maladjusted pupils.* London, 1965. See also: Mishne, J. Group therapy in an elementary school, *Soc. casework* (New York, Family Service Association of America), vol. 52, no. 1, 1971; Capul, M. *Les groupes rééducatifs.* Paris, P.U.F., 1969.

57. For an excellent study of residential treatment of very serious disturbance , see: Kahan, V. L. *Mental illness in childhood.* London, Tavistock, 1971. A striking experiment was carried out in a kibbutz with twenty-four severely disturbed, culturally deprived adolescent boys, involving an over-all environmental therapy proving that in a high proportion of very difficult cases severe mental disturbance is reversible even in the second half of the teens. See: Kohen-Raz, R. *From chaos to reality.* New York, Gordon & Breach, 1972.

58. In some cases, certainly, others may be involved; see Bissonnier, H. *Pédagogie de résurrection.* Paris, Fleurus, 1964. The author considers the contribution of religious education to the rehabilitation of the maladjusted.

59. Such evidence as we possess of the effectiveness of psychotherapy and other related forms of individual treatment is not very encouraging. Most studies claim 'improvement' in about two-thirds to three-quarters of children seen at child guidance clinics, but about the same proportions recover spontaneously. (See: Levitt, E. R. Psychotherapy with children—a further evaluation. *Behav. res. therapy* (Elmsford, N.Y.; Oxford, England), vol. I, pt. 1, 1963; and his earlier paper in *J. consult. psychol.* (Washington, D.C., American Psychological Association), vol. 21, 1953; Eysenck, H. J., ed. *Handbook of abnormal psychology.* London, Pitman, 1960, paper on 'The effects of psychotherapy'; Shepherd, M.; Oppenheim, A. N.; Mitchell, S. Childhood behaviour disorders and the child guidance clinic: an epidemiological study. *J. Child psychol. & psychiatr.* (Elmsford, N.Y., Association of Child Psychology and Psychiatry; Oxford, England), vol. 3, no. 1, 1966; and Tizard, J. Maladjusted children and the child guidance service. *London educ. rev.* (London, University of London Institute of Education), vol. 2, no. 2, 1973, p. 22–37.

60. Morse, W. C. Enhancing the classroom teacher's mental health function (*In*: Cowen, E. L., et al. *Emergent approaches to mental health problems.* New York, Appleton Century, 1967); and Morse, W. C. *School mental health programmes: source material.* Ann Arbor, Mich., University of Michigan, 1971.

61. See *Constructive education for adolescents* (the second volume of this work), chapter 8, for an examination of psychological and other services to schools.

62. Lodge, T. S. Research and research methods. *In*: Klare, H. J.; Haxby, D., eds. *Frontiers of criminology.* Oxford, Pergamon, 1967.

63. See also the earlier two volumes in this series.

Chapter six

An individual focus

ENVIRONMENT THE KEY

The children and young people so far dealt with in this book are, as a broad category, sometimes described as 'exceptional'. It would probably be better to use the word 'disadvantaged', in the sense that, either because of disability or damage in the child or because of environments which in some way or another are inadequate, deviant or defective, the normal processes of socialization and the interaction of maturation with the environment to bring about learning of all kinds have been made more than usually difficult for them. Many, even most, physical handicaps are as much givens in the equation of development as are such physical characteristics as skin or eye colour: little can be done to remove or fundamentally alter them, though something may be possible to palliate any restriction or disadvantage they may impose. But, in by far the majority of children and adolescents who conspicuously fall behind in school, develop emotional or behavioural difficulties, become delinquent in the true sense or have great problems in adjusting themselves to their surroundings at home, at school or at work, there is no evidence that they deviate in any marked way—physically or physiologically—from the normal. Their problems must be traced to faulty learning arising from some imbalance between their power to adjust and learn, and an environment which is in some way deficient or at least discrepant from their needs. Even where the handicap is a very severe impediment indeed and, like cerebral damage, enough by itself to account apparently for most or all of the difficulty in learning which we see, we cannot afford to be resigned. From all our knowledge of human learning we must assume that it is possible so to manipulate the environment that function will be improved over time.

This does not of course mean that, by suitable environmental help, all children can achieve some standard of general normality or be restored to that fullness of learning which they might have had were there no handicap. Nor does it mean that in every case the environment must be incriminated for all deficiencies in a child's learning or adjustment. Some children, without in any way being damaged, are genetically more vulnerable to upset than others, are less robust in their capacities to adjust, have perhaps less vitality, greater sensitivity, a higher or lower general strength of impulse, and so on. The normal variation in capacities of all kinds is very great. A similar range is found in environments: one that might fully meet the needs of one child might prove for another to be inadequate or even disastrous. We are thus engaged in the study of complex interactions which for most children work out satisfactorily but for some result in an accumulative mismatch and a series of increasingly faulty and deviant learnings. Hence, when things begin to go wrong or a child is manifestly disadvantaged by handicap, the main effort will have to be educational in the very broadest sense—a time-consuming, unspectacular, day-by-day task of seeing to it that the inputs of stimulation from the environment do, in so far as is possible, remedy any experiential deprivation which may have been caused by the handicap, correct any mislearnings and develop and strengthen the child's capacities to learn adequate ways of coping. What we must be concerned to achieve is the optimal level of functioning of which each individual child is capable—what is 'normal' for him or her.

The highly individual balance between the child's capacities to adjust and what the environment provides, expects or enforces, precludes the application of blanket programmes or techniques. Although there are superficial similarities in causes and in effects, all exceptional children are exceptional in ways which make each of them unique. Even those whose difficulties in learning or whose maladjustments seem to have no organic cause differ greatly from one to another in the ways in which their experiences or deprivations have interacted with their development to produce the situation as we see it when the child is first brought forward for attention. Moreover, as the process of education continues, the responses of each individual will to some very considerable extent be idiosyncratic. This uniqueness is, of course, a characteristic of each one of us. Where, however, learning and development are proceeding more or less normally, we tend to ignore the differences—at least in those situations where children are learning in some sort of a group, as they do in school. By and large, close inter-individual interaction (where most early learning takes place) is restricted for most children to the family or to a few friends and companions; and, as we know, the influence of the family is strongly prepotent over that of the school, as is probably that of the peer-group in late childhood and adolescence.

THE PRIMARY EDUCATORS

It follows that those who care intimately for a handicapped child—usually his parents—are, and continue to be at least over the first decade of life, the most important elements in any programme aimed at enhancing his general abilities and adjustment. The main role of the expert outsider is, through those directly in contact with the child, to bring about such changes in the intimate environment as make it more constructively adequate to the individual's needs. Specialized pedagogical and psychological treatments—psychotherapy, speech therapy, remedial education, behaviour modification and so on—are supplementary to what goes on between the child and his caretakers in all the highly charged emotional situations preceding and outside any formal education. This has been reiterated in different forms earlier in this book. It remains the key to any likelihood of real success. When we look closely at what is done in special education, however, we tend to find that such attention as is paid to parents and others in direct caring roles is, in practice, more of the nature of lip-service. The professional tends to take over as the main educator and the parent is relegated to second place or even ignored. Yet, any take-over is only likely to be successful if it is complete and the child is placed in a very small group in some sort of institution which fulfils all the educative roles. Such a solution may be unavoidable in some cases, particularly where the maladjustment in learning and in general personality development is a direct result of mishandling at home and the attitude and precipitating circumstances cannot be changed. It may also be necessary where the deficits and deprivations are such that a very specialized series of pedagogical techniques has to be applied over a very large part of the day—as for example in the case of the deaf-blind or children who have been exposed to extremes of neglect, cruelty and deprivation.

Such situations, although dramatic and therefore attracting much attention, are fortunately rare. For the most part, what is required is a modification in the out-of-school environment which can be brought about by a close and equal collaboration between the child's caretakers—usually the parents—and someone expert enough to understand both what is lacking or awry, and to be able to interact with the parents in such a way that they can first become aware of what is lacking or wrong and then learn to modify their behaviour and attitudes. What we are saying, in fact, is that the family must be treated as the primary educational unit, that the role of the expert is that of helping the family to find its own way and to solve its own problems. To this, special efforts directed to individual treatment in school or particular skilled attention to the child's own learning are secondary, even though in most cases they are important.

AN EXAMPLE

What is meant can be illustrated by the comparatively simple example of a child who is reading very badly, if at all, at, say, the age of 9. Closer examination of such a child usually reveals a constellation of adverse factors, no one of which could in any sense be held to be directly and uniquely causal, but which all together seem to be operating to depress the ability to learn, either generally or in the specific field of reading. Perhaps there has been some difficulty in establishing cerebral dominance which makes left-right tracking somewhat less easy to acquire; perhaps there is evidence of slight, even transitory, emotional disturbance—due to the death of a beloved grandparent, to a mother's illness or absence, to some family dissension—which has affected the power to concentrate; perhaps there is acute and depressing sibling rivalry with a smaller brother or sister who is earning praise all round for quickness in learning; perhaps at an important period for the development of speech the child was hospitalized and mother was able to visit only sporadically. The child may have a barely noticeable and undetected but chronic difficulty in vision or in hearing and simply not be seated close enough to the front of the class to hear or see easily what is going on. There may be a preoccupation with problems of acceptability to other children in the class and a sense of being picked upon by the teacher and rejected by peers.

There are, of course, cases of learning difficulty where apparent causal factors are much more dramatic than these, but there seem to be few indeed where one single cause can confidently be incriminated. What we tend to find is a combination of small or even more serious impediments acting, like straws on the proverbial camel's back, to make adjustment in the formal situations of school—even a warmly active infant school—more difficult than usual. Sometimes, the difficulties are even greater at home and school learning seems, initially, unaffected; but sooner or later the child begins to fall behind, in his or her social development, in relationships of all kinds, and in such things as mathematics or reading. Failure begins to predominate over success in one important area or in all; praise is rarer and rarer at home or in school. A self-image is built up which, in the face of any new task or challenge to adjustment, subtly indicates that failure is more likely than success. It can also be that, without realizing what they are doing, parents build up the notion that reading is a difficult business, that they had difficulties themselves or that it is not important anyway. On the other hand, when their child's failure becomes increasingly apparent, they may pile on the pressure, betray their anxiety by offering bribes, or curtail play time in the interests of home teaching.

IDIOSYNCRACY OF FAILURE

Failure to learn, whether in terms of the cognitive skills and other aspects of formal education or in the broad field of relationships or general social development, is intensely personal and idiosyncratic—just as, indeed, is success. It is one of the most striking facts to come from research that almost any combination of adverse factors may be associated with failure or be found in success: indeed, the only difference that can be fully established is that failing children have in their backgrounds, on the average, more adverse factors than do successful children—whether the failures are educational, failures in socialization (like delinquency or much maladjustment), or apparently due to some sort of handicap. We are in a situation where the pressures or deficits of an environment may or may not be matched by the resources that the individual can mobilize for himself—his assets, like general level of ability—or that can be mobilized for him by those who make up his human environment. If the threshold of difficulty is low and the resources reasonably high, then the balance will move to success; if the threshold of difficulty is high or the resources low, then failure will accumulate.

Very many children with considerable adverse factors in their environment or in their physical equipment do come through well and successfully. Some —and the statistics of handicap given earlier suggest how many—seem almost hopelessly starcrossed from birth. More (particularly among the educationally subnormal and the maladjusted) seem not to succeed in a struggle which is unequal only because an environment, sufficient for others to succeed, is not supportive enough for them.

The highly individual nature of the combination of personal and environmental circumstances which lies at the root of failure means that our study of a handicapped child, and any planning to help, must also be painstakingly individual. We cannot prescribe for groups, however they may be formed. Moreover, since in most cases a child does not come to attention until something is very wrong with his learning, there is nearly always a profound remedial job to do both with him and with his parents, a task prejudiced by unhelpful attitudes and deviant learnings built up over time—not infrequently with the connivance of services whose intention is to help. This added difficulty could be greatly minimized if those in contact with families from birth were more sensitively aware of the combinations of factors which constitute adverse environments, if they were watchful for the first signs of deviation in any child's development, and if all those social workers, district nurses, general practitioners and educational staff concerned with young children and their families were more fully acquainted with normal development in all its range of difference. Parents should certainly not be made unduly anxious, but there are many ways of interacting with them to improve their skills, to help them adapt the environment which they provide to any special need or weakness, to support them through difficulties and, particularly, to reassure them in their prime educational task. For this a warm, unsentimental stance on the part of the family counsellor is needed, an attitude which neither blinks at the problems nor arouses excessive guilt. And time and patience are necessary, particularly in those cases where some mild physical difficulty or general subnormality occurs in a child whose parents themselves are neither very intelligent nor well educated.

VULNERABLE POINTS

Crucially, such help is most concerned with what we might call the highly vulnerable points in development. In very early childhood—from birth to 3 years—normal children are developing their basic coping styles, their early attitudes to themselves and the world, and through their sensori-motor apparatus, essential fundamental concepts. They enlarge their life space by increasing mobility and come into contact increasingly with the prohibitions, explanations, facilitations and so on of their human environment; they learn a measure of impulse control, and ways of interacting successfully with others; they learn speech and a whole system of social communication; they acquire the basis of their security and confidence in themselves, their parents and other adults, and in the rationality and friendliness of the world. Anything that prejudices these processes of learning is going to accumulate prejudicial effects on subsequent development. Hence, any child for whom circumstances do not provide the means to these developments is at risk. Any handicap, physical or social, even if it is mild, can interfere; and often the damage is done not so much because the difficulty is ignored but because those around the child are unaware of the deprivation or difficulty which is being imposed upon him by, for example, a very slight hearing loss or a brief, but painful, period of hospitalization away from mother. Nor do they see that a disordered home, or a tired or discouraged mother, may be as much a threat to cognitive and affective growth as paralysed limbs.

The period immediately preceding entry to compulsory schooling is also a highly important one. Socialization in the first three to five years is almost uniquely the concern of the immediate family. Entry to playgroup, nursery school or first school means socialization into a wider and, in many ways, different group where comparisons become evident to the child and to his parents, and where aspects of a very different environment begin to affect a child. It is a transition too which, even for normally developing children, needs careful management. There are problems of acceptance and rejection by peers and by non-family adults—made difficult by disfigurements, for example, or by differences in expectation; there are problems of physical ability and competence in, for example, educationally important activities like construction, large body movements and even vocabulary. There is for the physically disabled the direct effect of treatments of various kinds involving interference with normal activities and development, likely to be more serious once very dependent early childhood is over and the child is more mobile and articulate. The burden upon mother coping with home, school and treatment, although she may accept it gladly, nevertheless influences her view of her child, particularly if he or she does not always fit smoothly and willingly into her arrangements. There are the attitudes, expressed in many subtle or overt ways, of other parents, other adults, of siblings and of other children, which for child and mother alike colour their view of the world and of each other.

It is frequently forgotten that by far the majority of children with some sort of handicap are educated in ordinary schools. It is mainly the dramatically and obviously physically damaged who are, in some sort, set apart for special attention early on. In most cases the handicap is slight, or is regarded as an 'inevitable' social, economic or environmental problem about which not much can be done. Such handicaps—minor sensory defects, developmental lags in speech, dulling of learning capacity by poor environment and so on—are either undetected or taken for granted until notice is drawn to them by the learning or personality problems which they generate; and this perhaps not until the end of the first school around the age of 8 when poor reading ability attracts a teacher's concern. The tendency with the more severely physically or sensorily handicapped has hitherto been to segregate them on the basis of the type of handicap. In some cases this is inevitable for very practical reasons; but it is doubtful whether this should always be so, and it could certainly be much less frequent than it is if we were to provide the resources necessary to make 'ordinary schools special'—something which would benefit not only the obviously damaged, but the much larger group of socially, mentally and mildly physically handicapped too. The resources required are of two kinds: the simple adaptations of premises and the provision of equipment; and the much more important provision of trained staff with time and skill to supplement what the ordinary school and its teachers can do to help the handicapped and disadvantaged in the classroom and to ensure the continuing educative interaction with the families.

REMEDIAL AND HELPING ROLES

It is this second area which presents the most difficulty. We still tend to believe that special help must be given exclusively by specially trained staff. We fail to exploit the fact that most human learning goes on in groups—between peers, between parents and children, in casual contacts for other purposes—rather than in formal learning situations presided over by specialists. Of course, there must be special help and teaching, and there must be teachers and others highly trained to do it. But this is not enough and, unless we are prepared to staff schools with experts at a very great density, is not likely to succeed by itself. What are needed are knowledgeable and humane teachers and others able to organize, inspire and support the natural educators who surround any child, showing them practically how, with relatively small modifications of existing circumstances, a truly constructive environment can be developed to support the disabled or disadvantaged in an effort to make headway against their difficulties. Since teaching and helping others is one of the best ways of learning for oneself, there can be little harm and much positive advantage in, for example, 'exploiting' some pupils to give help to others; and by improving one parent's skills in educating his or her own child one may prepare someone who can later on help others in the community.

Those, teachers and others, who are going to do this need a profound knowledge of handicap, of the dynamics of family life and of how human beings grow and learn. Thus the biggest difficulties are likely to lie in the training of expert staff and in inducing a change of role perception in professions like teaching, nursing, social work, psychology and medicine, which somewhat jealously guard their professional expertise, and a redefinition of the boundaries of their competence. But yet, that aspect of the mental health of communities which is related to all forms of handicap and disadvantage depends not on pity, not even upon compassion, but upon unsentimental understanding and effective help given as a matter of right and as an expression of acceptance of the value of difference. We cannot, ethically or economically, afford to have one child in five, perhaps even in four, developing at less than his best because our models of professional activity and roles are out of date.

ASSESSMENT

Any help we can give children and their families depends upon an accurate assessment of their difficulties in learning, of their assets and liabilities, and the development of a realistic programme of intervention over a considerable period of time. Such assessment and planning are not a matter of snap diagnosis, nor should they be confined to the kinds of learning usually associated with schooling. They must be concerned with the whole of development—social, affective and cognitive—and should involve actively all those dealing with any handicapped or disadvantaged child. As with any worthwhile investigation, one proceeds by setting up and testing hypotheses, experimenting and improving as one goes along and, as with any situation in real life which involves human beings with all their imperfections, it has to be accepted as a process involving a search for the best possible compromise, not only for the child but for his family, and in the light of the possibilities.

Initially one of the most important matters is to establish whether the developmental or learning difficulty springs from a true defect in the central nervous system, which is likely to be largely irremediable. This is by no means always easy, since many disturbances of attention, imperfections in impulse inhibition, difficulties in perceptual analysis (either visual or auditory), clumsiness in motor control, and so on, do not have detectable neurological correlates, and may have other than physical origins. Where, however, damage is demonstrable, it may have to be accepted as such and means found to minimize its effect as far as possible. In doubtful cases, it seems best to proceed on the assumption that the difficulty is (as it were) a learned one and attempt to ameliorate it by training, particularly since the processes of re-education of such aspects as poor impulse control, shortness or disturbance of attention span, and difficulties in tracking and sequencing are likely to be the same (though perhaps somewhat more effective) as they would have been if the origin of the difficulty were largely or purely physical.

A second area which needs close attention in the early stages of a study is the effect upon a child's learning of quite minor (and even more so of major) defects in hearing or sight. As we have seen, defects in vision or hearing which do not produce obvious difficulties—like a hearing loss transitorily associated with catarrhal affections of the ear occurring irregularly or chronically—can have severe consequences for speech development and for general cognitive growth if they occur early in life. Similarly, mild high-tone deafness may not be detected until, in the early stages of reading, a child fails to make vital sound distinctions. Visual weaknesses may lead to headaches, make attention to distant blackboards trying, or may interfere with the smooth development from percept to concept and so on. Many such defects are fairly readily remediable; but often remedy does not come until at least some damage has been done or some development prejudiced. Early paediatric screening locates many such cases but, unless detection is followed by efforts to minimize the impact of even a slight handicap on development, it is not as helpful as it might be.

We also need to be concerned with evaluating the effects upon a child's early learning and development of a motor handicap of any kind and particularly one affecting locomotion. How far has it hindered mobility and what (if any) effort has been made to compensate for the lack of stimulating experience, including the praise for physical feats? Here too marginal defects may be important for development out of all proportion to their medical severity. Poor early prehension or motor co-ordination will interfere with the young child's exploration of objects and of himself, perhaps prevent or slow down the kind of throwing away and retrieving activity which exercises and fixes such concepts as object-permanence. Mild visual or auditory handicap may make learning games like 'peep-bo!' unsatisfying. Lack of or uncertainty in cerebral dominance, clumsiness in gross or fine motor co-ordination and similar problems render life that much more difficult and less rewarding. Certainly later on in the pre- and early school period when a child is trying his hand at formal learning, such mild imperfections may interpose hindrances both in social integration with other more agile and adept children and in establishing the right-to-left sequence which is an important aspect of deciphering the printed page or of writing.

Another important area is that of speech. Again there are difficulties in adequate early differential assessment of the kinds and impact of speech difficulties. Some may be simple developmental lags which, with a little encouraging help, will disappear with time. Others reflect the impoverishment of the home environment; others are the signs of emotional disturbance. Yet others may be one of a number of symptoms of neurological disturbance or damage. Whatever the cause may prove to be, a deficiency, defect or derangement of speech is, as we have seen earlier, a serious impediment to social contacts particularly for the young child and will act as an increasingly serious impediment to his general learning. From our point of view, it is clearly necessary to remedy the speech problem itself as far as possible; but this alone is unlikely to be sufficient. Poor speech will have interfered with, or be a reflection of, other aspects of development, and it is important to understand what the effects of this may have been. How far has a speech defect or immaturity, for example, made the child a laughing stock, how far has it inhibited him in his contacts with others, given him an adverse view of himself, made it difficult for him to ask those questions on which so much of the early structuring of intelligence depends? How far, on the other hand, does it reflect a general deprivation of linguistic and probably other experience, a poverty of concepts and vocabulary, and thus a handicap in the early stages of learning to read?

In considering these matters and others like them, since the list above is far from exhaustive, we must not lose sight of the whole child in his family and in other important settings. Every single aspect has to be evaluated, at least in provisional ways, in terms of its meaning to him in relation to the total picture. Hence we need to assess as accurately as possible his present level of functioning; his general level of intelligence and learning ability; his level of social maturity; his physical capacities and the adjustments he has made; the circumstances of his home life, and its physical and economic possibilities; and the far more difficult and subtle aspects of parental and sibling attitudes, capacities, and feelings.

We also need to know something of how the child appears in different significant settings. It is sometimes surprising to see the child at home, dependent and lagging in many aspects of development, speaking baby talk maybe, and at the nursery school or play group where he shows a much greater independence and capacity to cope in at least some respects. Children, especially young ones, tend to respond differently to different people, even to different members of their family. Hence, while in a clinic or an observation room one may get a good, even an optimal, picture of what a child can achieve, this needs careful correction by observations in the more normal settings of daily life—and it is with the improvement of function in normal life that we are concerned.

HISTORY

Indeed, one might go somewhat further. Once we have eliminated or allowed for those handicaps which are strictly physical or physiological in their origins, then our principal concern is with the main and continuing theatres of the child's learning, that is to say primarily with the home as assessed in its quality and capacity as an educational environment, and then with other environments in which the child has learned or is learning. We need a very careful analysis of the family history and background, and of the child's own developmental story within it. We have to attempt to build up in detail as many as we can of the objective facts of his life so far. We have to try to assess what, at the various stages, he may have missed, what he or his parents may have felt or understood from what was happening and some tentative evaluation of the dynamics of the whole group, the ways in which it interacts, the feelings which it nourishes and of which it is ashamed, the impact upon it of current and past problems. Much of such a history will be to a degree factually inaccurate, certainly as to detail and possibly as to chronology. Some of the essential details can be, and of course should be, checked from the records of G.P.s and hospitals as far as possible. But equally important is it to recognize that the view which the family presents of itself, and the ways in which the facts may have been forgotten, ignored or remembered, provide clues to the emotional climate of a child's life and to the ideas of himself he has built up from others, matters crucially important to the process of helping him and his family to make the best possible job of his future development. They help us too to assess the possibilities of change in the family, in its attitudes, for example, or in its willingness and ability to undertake difficult readjustments of their ways of bringing up their child or their capacity to understand needs and to make compromises.

Much of what has been described is an expert and time-consuming task, and it is tempting to take short cuts in terms of what research has to tell us about broad causes or of what our experience has taught us with deceptively similar cases we have met before. When, as is true even in advanced countries, highly expert staff are few in number and costly to train, it may be a counsel of hopeless perfection to insist upon a thorough preliminary study of every handicapped child conducted by an expert.

But even here, it is well to remember two things. Much of what we need is simple factual material which almost any sympathetic listener trained to ask the right questions or working from a check list can obtain. But the process of gathering a history through talking to the family is also the beginning of that co-operative educative process of family involvement, and therefore some at least of the initial contact and study should be made by the person who will ultimately be the main liaison with the home. And this person will not necessarily be an expert professional.

Such a preliminary study is the beginning. It serves to provide us with some hypotheses—not with definitive diagnoses in most cases—as to likely factors contributing to the present state of affairs. These tentative hypotheses are worthless unless they are a starting point for some more enlightened attempt to improve the child's learning and whole circumstances. And it is this attempt, in the form of a diagnostic educational programme, which will test our hypotheses by the hard light of a child's progress towards the optimal adjustment for him.

THE ASSESSMENT AND PLANNING FUNCTION OF THE GROUP

Considered in this light, the role of expert diagnosis is more limited than we at first thought. Obviously the more strictly technical aspects of the study of a child have to be confided to experts—medical, psychological or social—and this, by and large, we contrive to do where services are reasonably adequate. But a very large part of the real task is not in this sense diagnostic or 'expert' at all. It is likely to be most effective, most useful for the child and his family, and most enlightening if it is based upon a learning experience developed by all those practically concerned. This is to say that at every stage of the study of a child, whether by psychologist, social worker, teacher, paediatrician or sympathetic lay person, every member of the team has a duty to engage in the mutual education of that team and to involve parents and others in contact with the child in the same educational activity. This is not a simple matter of telling others the findings or of seeking information from them. It depends on an attempt to evolve action hypotheses together, an effort at sensitization about what to look for, what sort of criteria to apply (and not merely the criteria of the specialist) for evaluating success, of eliciting suggestions with a clearly understood rationale for future action—in fact a group learning experience in which the different participants in different ways at different stages contribute on terms of full equality. Each participant in such a group will have a different role, while roles may change from time to time; nor is it likely or essential that they will meet together very often, if at all, as a total group. Some, for example the teacher concerned with the child, perhaps some older children and certainly the parents and maybe a social worker, will tend to be long-term members; others, the psychologist, the G.P., the speech therapist, may be *ad hoc* or short-term members only and will tend to slip back into roles of consultant, resources of information, suggesters of possible techniques, and so on, once the initial stages of intensive study have moved into the conduct over an extended period of a remedial or constructive programme.

At critical points, there will be difficult decisions as to appropriate compromise courses of action to be taken. There will also be a framework of recording, of testing progress against agreed criteria, of goal setting and goal modification—all of which in their several ways have to be a collective decision accept-able to those who have to carry them out or apply them. Hence it is likely to be most valuable to have from the outset some knowledgeable person to act as a general co-ordinator of all the activities that affect the child and his family. This could very well be a teacher specialized in handicap work attached to an ordinary school or to a group of schools receiving handicapped children. But, with suitable support and some training, it could be an experienced parent or other adult working semi- or entirely voluntarily.

PLANNING AND CONDUCT OF EDUCATION

In a necessarily schematic and chronological way we can attempt to indicate how this might work out in practice. Clearly the first and in some ways the most delicate step is that of conducting the initial case study described above. This will be the basis for a meeting at which the results will be fed back and for raising the questions which occur not only to the professionals concerned but most importantly to the parents. These questions may either lead to the search for further information, be the basis of the first-treatment hypotheses or indicate areas of anxiety or guilt, and bring them out for examination. Even if such a case conference occurs at an early stage in the child's life, before the age of compulsory schooling, it would be wise to draw into it those who will be concerned with the child in nursery or primary school. By the time the child is ready for nursery or primary school, and still more at any later educational stage, the inclusion of the head and class teacher is essential since, next to the parents, the child's teacher is the most important person in his education.

The objects of this first stage are numerous. We have first to ensure that whatever can be done to palliate the effects of any physical disability is done, and in such a way as to interfere as little as possible with the smooth progress of the child's development on the cognitive, affective and social levels. This may well involve ingenious compromises between strictly medical and physical needs on the one hand, and the psychological needs of the child on the other. Nor should we neglect the effects of intervention or non-intervention upon the parents and their ability to provide a satisfactory home experience or to arrange for the child to attend a school or treatment centre. It is important that decisions of this kind are recognized by all concerned as being inevitably of the nature of a compromise in which expertise, experience and understanding are pooled to come to a consensus to which the parents are fully a party—particu-larly since the consequences of any decision are likely to be most felt by them and, short of quick and dramatic physical interventions, it is on what they are able to do full-heartedly that the success of any measure will depend. In a very real sense the outsiders should make available to the family their expertise; they should not persuade but help the family to take its own decision, evoking from parents and siblings, who have been made truly acquainted with the difficulties and the likely outcomes, their own freely expressed conclusions. This, it should be emphasized, is not likely to be a brief process in which factual information is conveyed by experts and acted upon in highly rational ways by families. All parents have strongly emotional attitudes to their children; they can rarely be detached; and those whose children have some kind of handicap or developmental difficulty are often overwhelmed by and ashamed of fears and anxieties for their child and for themselves. Some will wish to adopt a highly dependent 'you know best' attitude; some will find it difficult even to accept that their child is any different from others or has any special need; yet others will be aggressive, tending to project their guilt onto the experts or the services which they feel have let them down; some will attempt to manipulate the services to their own immediate advantage or to enhance their prestige, or try to get a face-saving label; and some, the most difficult of all, may be so entangled in their own neuroses that they project them onto the child and blame him for their own difficulties. None of these attitudes will be changed rapidly nor will they be altered by authoritative statements. Any change will come about only slowly through a process which respects a parent's decisions, and supports them so far as is possible and acceptable, even if to the professional they seem wrong. In this early stage, there is clearly a process of establishing trust between the family and the outsiders, a process of gaining confidence which can only be built lastingly—even in the case of the most depressed and difficult parents—on the basis of respect. And such respect does not mean allowing oneself to be manipulated any more than it does between, say, parent and child. It is based upon professional integrity, in making clear what one thinks and why, what the alternatives are and what are the likelihoods of success attached to each—all this as objectively and as fully as possible, but in such a way that the caring nature of the relationship is never in any reasonable doubt.

It is in such a climate of trust and caring that the whole matter should proceed in group meetings from time to time or in individual contacts. We need, for example, to assess what sorts of deprivation and difficulty have been imposed upon the child by his handicap. This is obviously a delicate area to raise with parents because they readily perceive themselves as having been inadequate or neglectful, or at the best unimaginative; or it may be that they simply do not understand that physical care by itself is insufficient. It can readily be seen that the approach most likely to succeed is one in which the necessary information on child growth is conveyed simply and unemotionally in terms a parent can understand, and then followed by an invitation to the family—other children if they are old enough as well as mother and father—to devise ways whereby they can put this information to practical use in helping their own sibling or child. In this kind of process, the experience of other parents who have had the same or complementary difficulties can be extremely useful since they are likely to appear both more sympathetic and less threatening than any professional. Additionally, they can often demonstrate the 'how to do it'—for example, the modifications they have made in their own homes, the toys which they have invented and how they use them—show the routines they have found serviceable as well as discuss from personal knowledge some of the feelings they have experienced.

KEY IMPORTANCE OF THE TEACHER

Once the child is in some sort of school, many things become more readily possible than when all the work has to be carried out in brief visits to the home or clinic or through *ad hoc* groups. In nursery class, play group or infant school there is someone, not the parent, with knowledge and experience of the development of normal children. The teacher, particularly if he or she has a complement of special training, is well fitted for two very critical tasks. The first and most obvious is what might be called diagnostic teaching; the exploration of the child's learning difficulties of all kinds as they show up in situations more real than those of testing in a clinic or laboratory. Such a teacher can, for example, observe very carefully and record the child's speech as it is used in the social situations of school—a valuable set of observations which complement the study made by a competent speech therapist and the kind of information given by a parent. It is also possible to see how some defect in perception actually hinders learning, or how the child may be developing strategies of his own to overcome it. Finally, in consultation with the psychologist, the teacher can set up exploratory learning programmes devised according to the hypotheses arising from a knowledge of the child, and see how far these are borne out in practice and how far the initial tentative estimates of cause have to be revised in the light of experience. In actually helping the handicapped, from whatever cause, it is rarely sufficient to devise and pursue a strategy based upon an initial examination, even if that has been thorough. It is of great importance that the teacher rests responsive to what actually happens as the child learns and develops, and changes tactics and expectations accordingly.

A teacher who is conducting work with a handicapped child along these lines is in a very good position to co-operate directly with the child's parents and to evolve with them modifications in the child's home life which will support and extend whatever is being done in school, to consult with them as to whether some effect or change noticeable at school is also observable at home, to suggest that they try out with their child some new form of specific activity and to review over-all progress with them from time to time.

This form of direct parent–teacher co-operation, coming about naturally and almost spontaneously, provides a vector for another and equally important aspect of the remedial and constructive programme. It will tend, of course, to enhance the parents' skills in a direct way and thus multiply the effects of teaching. Because they are doing something meaningful for their child, it will bring child and parent closer together. But an insightful teacher can do more, particularly if he or she is fully in the confidence of the other professionals: she can, in fact, and indirectly, 'treat the family' as a whole unit, reinforcing many of those intangible attitudinal and behavioural changes on which success ultimately depends.

Since, next to the parents and in a somewhat more public and detached way the teacher is the person most directly in contact with the handicapped child, it seems sensible that he or she should be the anchor of the whole treatment team, helped perhaps by a suitable volunteer parent or indeed supporting discreetly such a helper in discharging the whole co-ordinating role. He or she should discharge many of the co-ordinating and record-keeping tasks which the maintenance of an active and evolving educational programme over a period of years must entail. This is something which even teachers regarded as fully trained in the field of special education have not been equipped to do; nor, for that matter, has any other professional involved. But because of the central position of education in dealing with all forms of handicap in the first two decades of life, it seems that teaching rather than social work or medicine should be the main source of recruitment for staff to discharge this responsibility. Economically—both in terms of time and in terms of training—it seems more viable than adding yet another social worker to family services which are mainly oriented to crisis intervention rather than to the longer-term, more truly educational objectives of making the best of what we have.

UNDERSTANDING OF OBJECTIVES

Research in many remedial and general educational fields indicates that some sort of structure of objectives apparent to the teacher and to the taught, some systematic setting, evaluation and resetting of goals, is an important ingredient in success. It is important to know what we do and why, if we need to evaluate our success and change our tactics as soon as failure threatens. It is useful, therefore, both when work is begun with a child with a learning difficulty or a disability, and from time to time as the work proceeds, to set down our hypotheses systematically, to record our objectives as we see them, to detail the strategies which we propose to use, to note what it is that is expected from (and agreed to by) each of those involved. This should not, of course, be a rigid series of prescriptions to be adhered to through thick and thin, but a kind of map; one at least of the purposes of which is to lay bare in advance the points of difficulty so that we may be prepared and plan for them. Such a plan should indicate the weighing of probabilities against desirability, should attempt to lay down some agreed priorities for the child, for his parents, for his other educators, in strictly functional terms concerned with the costs in terms of time and effort, of possible disappointment and its emotional effects. It should be realistic, but with some considerable tinge of optimism, and it should be frequently reviewed in the light of accumulating knowledge of the individual child's development, of the impact of events on the family, and so on. Such an over-all plan will necessarily be at least in part in vague terms and it should be supplemented—for all those engaged in the daily business of helping the child along the road to optimal functioning—by a series of plans covering much shorter spans. These would indicate to whoever would be most actively concerned—for example the area of competence (which might be an aspect of reading or mathematics or some development in social skills) to which special attention is to be directed for, say, a fortnight or a month. In devising such plans we need to list the child's current assets, what he knows or has achieved along the lines we wish him to go—what some psychologists would call his 'entry behaviours'. We then need to look at the other end of the process and list, realistically, the desired outcomes in performance, behaviour, social skills, attitudes or whatever it is that is of immediate relevance to our over-all programme. We should then be in a position to suggest what forms of teaching, or of experiences, what modifications in routines, what treatments and so on will help us and the child to the attainment of the objective, who will carry them out and by what criteria we shall be able to judge along the way and, at the end, how far we have progressed towards the goals.

The devising of such a schema may reveal, for example when we are listing the child's initial entry behaviours and assets, that there are serious gaps which we have tended to overlook but which have to be remedied before we can embark on what we want to do. It may also show us that there are very real choices of objectives or of methods to be employed or that very serious thought has to be given as to who—parent, teacher, another child or some combination of people—will carry out the interactive processes which are implied. It should reveal to us also the points at which we should pause and take stock (and by what means this should be done) to see whether the expected progress is being made. And we should accompany such a short-term plan by some form of recording.

Two matters are more pertinent here than they seem at first sight. The devising of short-term plans in this way is neither a magical formula or ritual nor is it of course the whole of education. The projected outcomes will not be the whole of the result and, indeed, one must expect both welcome and unwelcome and, in any case, unexpected outcomes. What such planning does, however, is to make one alert to processes and outcomes and able rapidly to exploit those which are useful. It will also make diagnostic teaching more enlightening and effective since each plan and each evaluation alerts all those concerned to the need for some reformulation every now and then of aspects of the child's progress and problems.

Perhaps the most important aspect, however, is the potential use of such plans in the ongoing education through involvement of the child and of his parents. Just as we have insisted that parents and, so far as is possible, children themselves should be brought into an equal and co-operating relationship in the development of long-term plans and in all important decisions, so it is important that at least the child should be continuously a party to his own learning. This means that the educator, whether this happens to be the teacher, the parent, some untrained helper or another child, must not only be a party to the setting up of objectives and have a real understanding of the methods to be used, but must share a commitment to them with the learner. Schemas such as we are suggesting are in some sort 'negotiated contracts', not matters imposed by teacher or taught. Among other things, this means that, as far as it is possible to do so, the learner (child, parent, helper or teacher) takes part in the planning process, in the assessment of own performance towards the goal, and helps to set and reset targets as work proceeds. Clearly, because we wish to maintain an involvement of all the child's educators in his progress through their daily contacts with the child, this imposes upon the professionals in any team an effort to make clear to all concerned what the objective might realistically be, what the choices are and in what directions the whole process is tending. It is important, too, that those involved know just what is expected of them, where to get support when their heart fails them and how far any lack of success is due to unrealistic target setting, to an attempt at a forlorn hope, to a defective method or to a human failing in themselves.

MALADJUSTED CHILDREN

In what has been said in this chapter so far, somewhat greater stress has been laid upon the problems of those children whose learning difficulty is primarily related to some form of physical handicap or disability, though most of the principles apply to other groups and individuals. Those children who become maladjusted because of circumstances in their family lives, and those whose early environment has inhibited the fullest possible development of their general ability to learn, present in many respects a more difficult remedial and constructive problem, as do those handicapped children whose home circumstances are far from ideal. In such cases only too often the causes lie in the inadequacy (for a great variety of reasons) of the child's primary and most important educators—the parents. The task is not simply that of involving otherwise caring and good parents in a process of self-education so that they can acquire the special skills and insight necessary to enhance whatever positive assets their child may possess, and to palliate the effects of damage or deficiency in physical mechanisms. We may have to engage in a much more profound remedial task—that of attempting to change radically some important aspects of the personalities of adults who may themselves be profoundly emotionally damaged or grossly inadequate. At the very least, we have so to change their everyday behaviours that the interaction with their children is not profoundly damaging.

In some cases, such a profound change is virtually impossible and there is little hope other than that of putting the child into another environment. In many more, the best that we can hope for is so to arrange things that as much as possible of the damaging effects of the system of relationships at home is neutralized, while trying to ensure that other educational environments, notably those provided by schools, are positively supportive. The hope would be that we can hold the line until adolescence weans the child away from dependence on the family and perhaps allows normal processes of growth and development to assert themselves, at least to the point that he or she comes to an adjustment tolerable to himself and others.

Essentially such a course involves strengthening and enriching the *milieu* outside the home—providing supportive and tolerant groups, small knots of determined 'friends' at school. A permissive, accepting but firm teacher who understands the source and cause of a child's difficulty, and is prepared to tolerate but not condone bad actions and feelings, to accept the child, reward effort, help in bearing the consequences of his failures, and explain why he is as he is and propose ways in which he can learn to make more effective adjustments in relationships or behaviour, will often carry a maladjusted individual through the danger points of childhood and adolescence without deep and permanent damage. This is particularly likely to be so if the relationship with the teacher or other adult can be reasonably permanent and non-possessive and if, so far as is practicable, the same careful and realistic planning of a broad strategy based upon careful study and supplemented by shorter-term and more detailed plans is employed as was suggested above. In some cases too there may be advantage in direct, special and personal help such as behaviour therapy or even psychotherapy, though neither of these alone is likely to be successful.

In many cases of maladjustment, as we have said, little can be done to change the family situation to the point where we can be sure of even moderate success. This is not, however, true of all, and probably is not even true of the majority, even of those families whose children show quite severe maladjustments. In not a few cases, the problem has arisen in reaction to a lengthy period of family crisis and the child's reactions to this have evoked responses from the parents which have, as it were, become locked into a mutually maladjusted relationship enduring long after the crisis has passed. In others it would hardly be true to say that the home environment was in itself truly maladjusted, but a combination of circumstances, perhaps for example over-protection or too high expectations at home with a school situation and a peer group intolerant of peculiarities, has led to the child developing coping styles which increasingly lead him into failures in relations, in school work and so on. The variety is endless and the degrees of severity equally so.

In such cases, the outlook for work with the family is generally hopeful; and sometimes all that is required is a little counselling with parent or teacher or both. In others, there may have to be quite a lengthy period of interaction with the family and with the child as a means of helping them to come to terms with and change their own attitudes and expectations, to understand something of the dynamics of their own conduct—or at least of the effects which it is likely to have on other people. Again, except in a few cases either of very young children or of those parents and children who are completely inaccessible to reasonable discussion, we may insist that it is unlikely that something done to an individual will in and by itself have much lasting effect. The family and the child have in some sort to wish to change, to be involved in devising their own goals and strategies of help, to engage in a learning, or rather a relearning, process, the aims and methods of which they at least consent to but preferably find for themselves with the help of a psychological counsellor. Moreover, since maladjustments have in general arisen in and are being sustained by an environment, it is to the environment as a whole that we must address ourselves, both at school and at home; if we cannot improve the learnings in these situations, then various 'therapies' are likely to achieve little.

None of this is simple, whether we are dealing with a handicapped, deprived, maladjusted or delinquent child. Success depends upon a sensitive assessment at the outset both of the child and of the immediate possibilities of his environments, a continued evaluation of progress and very careful planning. These can be described. But the whole enterprise turns upon how far the human skills of educating the various actors in the individual's environment can be successfully brought to bear so that parents, teachers, the child's own brothers, sisters and peers become in very important ways themselves the active agents of the remedial, compensatory and constructive tasks. Expert psychological, medical and educational knowledge is certainly necessary. It constitutes the basis on which we can realistically set proximate and long-term objectives and assess the probabilities of the success of any efforts we make. But although scientific understanding is clearly necessary, it is far from being sufficient. It has to be fed into a complex and sometimes unconsciously resistant system. It has to act as a catalyst for changing relationships and attitudes in such ways that the professional's knowledge and understanding is willingly and actively transformed into the actions and feelings of the child himself, his parents, brothers, sisters, friends and teachers.

CONCLUSION—FULL CIRCLE

We have now come full circle in the sense that a community's mood, particularly that of a community undergoing the stresses of change, is a function of each individual's mental health in the various group settings of which he is a part. The problem of exceptional children—the one in four or five who represent the casualties of our system—is merely that of all children, writ somewhat larger perhaps and in a more challenging form. It is not so much a matter of removing stress, unless it is manifestly intolerable, but of so strengthening the personality that children and young people can triumph over it and so learn even more powerful coping styles. In doing this we are, above all, occupied with the child's primary educators—the family—and with the school as a secondary but very important *milieu* which has the advantage that it is presided over by professionals who can consciously manipulate their own actions and various aspects of the environment they provide. Helping a maladjusted child to adjust to himself and others, re-educating a delinquent so that he does not need the delinquent behaviour, teaching a physically handicapped child to evolve ways of achieving fulfilment in work and leisure, are, like education in its broadest sense, based upon freeing the individual from acquired constraints so that he can continue to develop positively, can in confidence of success embark on a chain of learnings each of which is a provisional step in the maintenance of dynamic equilibrium—the kind of power to adjust, with some creative difficulty and anxiety perhaps, to that constant challenge of change which is what living in an evolving society is all about.

Appendix

SPECIAL EDUCATION NEEDS
Report of the Committee of Enquiry into the Education of Handicapped Children and
Young People.
London: Her Majesty's Stationery Office. Cmd. 7212, May 1978.

As was mentioned in the prefatory note to this volume, in the last decade there have
been few comprehensive attempts anywhere in Europe or North America to review the
entire field of provision for handicapped children and to determine a global policy. The
above Report is the only one which could be said to be a truly national attempt to study
the field in depth, and to propose major changes in the legal frameworks and the
structure of national and local provision, although there has been a mixture of partial
attempts, some governmental, some by voluntary bodies, and references to these will be
found elsewhere in this volume. In the UK this is the first enquiry of its kind since 1899.

The Committee of Enquiry on Special Educational Need was set up by the Secretary
of State for Education and Science (UK) under the chairmanship of a philosopher, Mrs
H. M. Warnock. It was widely representative of concerned professionals and laymen, of
official and voluntary bodies, industry, parents and even former pupils. It received over
400 submissions of evidence, commissioned five surveys[1] of practice and opinion, and
visited institutions in the UK, North America, Scandinavia, West Germany and Holland. It began its work in 1974, and reported in 1978.

The Report is certainly comprehensive, and covers all aspects of special educational
provision, from the child's earliest days to further and higher education and the transition to work. The focus is on the child in all his settings—home, school, leisure and
work—and it sees that, while many professions other than those strictly concerned with
education have important parts to play, the main thrust of all provision must be
educational in the widest possible sense. It must be concerned to foster the most
favourable growth of the individual, whatever his handicap may be.

This breadth of view, which concurs with the principles set out in this volume, stems
from another important statement of principle. The Warnock Committee proposes that
categories of handicap (like blind, deaf, motor handicap) should be abandoned, and no
longer have legal force. It insists, as I have done throughout, that there is little direct
relation between a more or less medical or physical diagnostic category and any learning
or development difficulty. It notes that we are faced with a continuum of learning
difficulties, the severity or nature of which may have only a tenuous relation with, for
example, the severity or even the kind of handicap. Some severely physically handicapped children may have learning difficulties which require prolonged and continuous
special educational help which can only be given in a special school or class. And so may
some whose physical handicap is slight. But by far the majority of the one in five or six of
all children needing some help will be able to get this effectively within ordinary
schools—and of these some may have major physical or sensory impairment. The report
does, however, propose to retain the term 'maladjusted', and a sub-category for children
with *specific* learning difficulties.

Thus the Committee sets its face firmly against both labelling and all that that implies
of separateness, and against the traditional classifications which, it points out, are
largely medical in origin, imply a medical model of 'treatment', ignore the developmental and educational aspects and tend to suggest that one profession has an exclusive or
overriding responsibility for diagnosis and care. The effect of its recommendations is to

[1] Of which by far the most generally useful is Cave, C. and Maddison, P., *A Survey of Recent
Research in Special Education*. Slough, NFER, 1978.

bring all children who fail to learn adequately under close and careful educational and psychological surveillance.

Consequently, the Report insists upon the responsibility of all professions and services which touch upon the child and his family—educational, social and medical—to co-operate in case-finding, examination, assessment and follow-up. This, it points out, has important consequences for training. All professions—medical and paramedical staff, social workers and all members of the education services—need to be sensitized to learning difficulty, developmental difficulty and handicap. It urges'that this should be an essential part of the basic training of teachers and other educators, psychologists, doctors, nurses and social workers, whatever their ultimate field of practice. Those whose work brings them into *close* contact with children and young people with learning difficulty (of whatever kind) need more thorough training, probably at a post-initial training-level, and to ensure the kind of interdisciplinary co-operation which is a major recurring theme of the report as much as possible of this should be given in training courses common to members of the different professions. Finally, the Report has much to say about the training at an advanced level of those who will be professionally and expertly concerned with diagnosis and assessment, with helping teachers and parents to provide the specially adapted education which such children may require at home, in school (ordinary or special) and in their further education and training.

The Report recognizes that the process of diagnosis is much more than a snapshot physical investigation, or even a psychological one. It should be based as much upon observation extended in time of how the child learns as upon particular deficits, and should lead to a carefully constructed profile on which a clearly defined programme of help is to be based. In this process of assessment and planning for the child or young person's future, the Committee assigns important parts not only to specialized professionals from psychology, education, medicine and social work, but to the child's teacher and head teacher and to the parents. It also stresses the necessity to maintain flexibility. Diagnosis and assessment are of the nature of hypothesis-making, leading to a provisional educational plan. Both plan and assessment should be reviewed at regular intervals, to monitor developments which might imply a change of tactics.

In line with its stress upon the primacy of education in its broad sense, the Committee assigns to parents a crucial role in fostering the development of their child. It is for this reason that it dwells upon the right of parents to be consulted, to give their agreement to whatever plan is devised for the child and to have access to the information about him gathered in the process of assessment—whilst, of course, preserving a necessary minimum of professional confidentiality. This accent upon the critical importance of the parents' role and responsibility for much of the education of their own child leads to some clear statements concerning the need to educate the parents themselves, especially in the very early months and years of the child's life, to provide for them a continuing link with the specialized educational, medical and social services through a 'named person', and to ensure that all the professionals with whom they or their offspring come into contact are sensitively aware of the complex of problems which surrounds handicap and learning difficulty.

In view of these basic concepts of learning difficulty and disorder, of the joint and equal responsibility attributed to parents and educators aided by psychological and medical experts, the Report's notions of how an adequate service should be set up are somewhat surprising. It suggests that so far as the educational services are concerned, this should be the responsibility of a special group of advisers in the local educational authority service (who correspond in some aspects of their status and functions to the inspectorate in other countries). It is true that the Committee recommends that such advisers should have had experience of work with handicapped children. What it does not specify is that they would need a very full and specialized training in educational psychology, including those skills of individual examination and study of children, skills with parents and so on, which form an essential part of the training of the educational psychologist. It proposes, in effect, a new service, and that in a country which already has in most places well-developed school psychological services working in the classrooms alongside teachers, parents and others, and directly and principally concerned with children with learning difficulties, maladjusted children and those who, for family reasons, have some temporary disturbance. The Report thus provides one more example of the sorry tendency to recommend a new and competing service to deal with a developing need, instead of looking at what exists and strengthening and widening it to meet an extension of its customary tasks.

In view of the Warnock Committee's insistence upon interprofessional and interdisciplinary co-operation it seems strange to wish to set up such an additional organization where there are already so many partial ones. The solution advocated in the present work[2] seems a much more effective way to ensure that all children with learning difficulties and their parents get the help which they need in as flexible and open a way as possible.

[2] *Constructive Education for Adolescents*. Chapter 8, and this volume, Chapter 6.

Subject Index